# Advanced Reading Skills

**Robert A. Snow**

District Administrator for Curriculum and Instruction
Somerville, Massachusetts, Public Schools

Author of *Reading Skills*

Mark McGowan

*When ordering this book, you may specify:*
*either* **R 604 W** *or Advanced Reading Skills*

**AMSCO SCHOOL PUBLICATIONS, INC.**
315 Hudson Street / New York, N.Y. 10013

As an English and reading teacher at both the secondary and elementary levels in Massachusetts, Robert Snow has taught thousands of students. As well, Mr. Snow has served as department chair and curriculum director. He has been a guest lecturer at the university level at Wheelock College, and he is a frequent director of workshops in the New England area for K–12 staff and parents.

*This book is dedicated with love and affection to*
*my daughter, Colleen, and my son, Christopher.*

Please visit our Web site at:

*www.amscopub.com*

ISBN 978-1-56765-006-8
*NYC Item 56765-006-7*

7  8  9  10  11  12    09  08  07

# PREFACE

*Advanced Reading Skills* provides a precise skill-by-skill approach to reading improvement with supplemental critical thinking and learning activities. Students discover how to identify and learn the basics of each of the twenty critical reading skills and apply those skills to thinking and learning activities in each unit. Students can apply their understanding of each skill in the content area subjects of language arts, social studies, and science, guided by precisely focused questions and activities. Thinking and learning activities serve the process of reviewing, integrating, and applying the skills in independent or cooperative group activities.

Active involvement is the key idea. There is nothing passive about this program. Students must read, think, and write in practical reading activities in several school subjects to develop skills that apply to those school subjects.

## Organization

Organization arises from the reading skills and the integration of the skills into thinking and learning activities across all subjects. (Form follows function.) There are twenty skills grouped into six instructional units.

   I. Context and Meaning Skills
  II. Technical Comprehension Skills
 III. Organizational Pattern Skills
 IV. Interpretive Critical Thinking Skills
  V. Higher Order Critical Thinking Skills
 VI. Study Skills

In each unit, students proceed in the following sequence:
▶ **Overview the Skills.** An introduction and demonstration of the skills.
▶ **Practice the Skills.** A reading selection provides student practice of each skill.
▶ **Applying the Skills in Content Subjects.** Selections are provided in the following order for practicing the skills:
    Language Arts Practice A, B, C
    Social Studies Practice A, B, C
    Science Practice A, B, C
    (The A-B-C selections indicate a slight increase in maturity of topic, application of skills, and, to a certain extent, readability levels. The readability

> levels for all selections average 9.0 through 12.0 according to the Fry Readability Formula.)

▶ **Thinking and Learning Activities.** Integrated activities for developing critical thinking skills within, beyond, and about the selections. Students can work independently, in cooperative groups, or together as a class.

## Methods for Individual Use

**Entire Program.**  Most students can benefit from proceeding through the entire program, unit by unit, practicing applying skills in each selection of each unit.

*Note:* In doing the questions for each selection, students should refer to the selections as needed. This is called "aided recall," and it reinforces the reading skills, especially the more detailed or technical ones. It also reinforces test-taking practice and process.

**One Subject Level.**  Reading profiles of students might indicate that it would be inappropriate for some students to proceed through the entire program. Content subject teachers may want to practice only the language arts or social studies or science selections. Their students might gain more by proceeding through just the specific content subject selections for language arts or social studies or science. However, other students may gain more by proceeding through all the A, B, or C selections, staying on one level throughout.

**Specific Skills.**  Other students, in view of their reading profiles, may benefit from concentrating on specific reading skills within the unit set in each selection.

## Thinking and Learning Activities

Each unit contains three sets of Thinking and Learning Activities: *Within a Selection, Beyond a Selection, About a Selection.* These activities provide for integrated application of the skills to develop critical thinking, research, writing, interdisciplinary, and test-taking skills.

The activities for *Within a Selection* and *Beyond a Selection* are modeled after Bloom's Taxonomy for Higher Order Thinking. This model provides six levels of the thought process: Knowledge, Comprehension, Application, Analysis, Synthesis, and Evaluation. Phrased as action verbs (Know, Comprehend, Apply, Analyze, Synthesize, Evaluate), these levels of thinking serve as headings to identify each activity, thus giving students clear-cut direction and goals. It is also important to note how the skills and critical thinking processes are practiced "Within a Selection," and then applied in real world situations in "Beyond a Selection."

**About a Selection**  provides opportunities for students to apply skills, thinking, and organization to working on projects and interdisciplinary units that involve research and writing. These Thinking and Learning Activities should be used appropriately for both measuring student abilities and integrating skill objectives. All units contain an equal number of six activities in the "Within" and "Beyond" sections. As the text progresses, a variety of activities is offered for reasons of integration, choice, and teacher planning for group activities in the "About" activities.

## Curriculum, Instruction, Assessment

Current theory and research in education speak to a balance in: curriculum—what is taught; instruction—how material is taught; assessment—how learning is measured. *Advanced Reading Skills* provides for a balance of quantitative measurement in the skills of each selection and qualitative measurement in the Thinking and Learning Activities. Teachers and students should work toward a balance of the two, and recognize that many state assessment programs now provide "open-ended" inquiry questions to measure thinking ability.

Also, the new Scholastic Aptitude Test will be primarily a critical reading skills test in the SAT—I Verbal Reasoning Test, and a critical writing skills test in the SAT II—Writing Test.

Teachers and students should find this text useful for informal preparation for both new state assessment tests and Scholastic Aptitude Tests, both verbal and writing sections.

## The Reading Selections

The selections present a balance of different kinds of writing: instructional (giving directions), narrative (storytelling), descriptive (describing), and expository (explaining, persuasive—and sometimes opinionated). All of these writing types are presented in the variety of content subjects—language arts, social studies, and science—to provide the student with reading and writing skills in the content subjects. The selections are models of concise and effective writing, with some excerpted from the world of literature and daily media. The topics are intended to capture the interest of the student, while improving skills.

Each selection also contains a "strategic reasoning" introduction (Prereading) that provides a short piece of information or question to brief the student about the topic in the selection.

## Extending the Use of the Selections

*Advanced Reading Skills* provides many questions and activities for improving reading comprehension, critical thinking, and writing ability. In addition to each unit, the following are available for appropriate use in each selection to further enhance the learning experience through integration of skills.

*Note:* Teachers are encouraged to develop a portfolio of student accomplishments from each unit, especially from the Thinking and Learning Activities in each unit and from the following suggestions. Such a portfolio represents ways to measure student abilities in a qualitative manner.

1. Explain the problem presented in the selection and one realistic solution.
2. Compare the selection to a current news event.
3. Apply the selection to your own life. How does it affect your life or why does it not affect your life or under what circumstances would it affect your life?
4. How does the selection impact your neighborhood or state or country?
5. Research the selection or the topic for a report or presentation.

6. Explain a personal experience that relates to the selection.
7. Choose a book or magazine article for comparison and contrast to the selection or topic.
8. Choose a movie or television program for comparison and contrast to the selection or topic.
9. Present your point of view about the selection or the topic.
10. Critique the selection.

## The Answer Key

Finally, the Answer Key (a separate pamphlet) serves as a guide. Some answers are either right or wrong because the skill questions are literal. Other answers are not quite as exact because the questions are more interpretive or inferential. Still other answers ask you to "choose an appropriate answer" because several choices are possible, depending on one's viewpoint.

## A Final Word

*Advanced Reading Skills* provides practical reading experiences to assist in developing comprehension, critical thinking, and writing skills consistent with current research in reading instruction and student learning. These experiences and skills are integrated into content subjects and expand the comprehension process into many activities for student participation.

This comprehension and thinking process is ongoing. It requires instruction, practice, review, and practical application. It is hoped that you will find a significant place for these lessons to provide both improved reading progress and enhanced learning environments for your students.

# CONTENTS

UNIT I  **CONTEXT AND MEANING SKILLS**
Overview the Skills      1
*Following Directions*
*Vocabulary Through Context Clues*
*Locating Facts and Answers*
*Sentence Meaning*

Practice the Skills      4
Applying the Skills in Content Subjects      6
*Language Arts, Social Studies, Science*
Thinking and Learning Activities      21


UNIT II  **TECHNICAL COMPREHENSION SKILLS**
Overview the Skills      23
*Major and Minor Topics*
*Main Idea and Topic Sentence*
*Details*
*Signal Words*

Practice the Skills      27
Applying the Skills in Content Subjects      29
*Language Arts, Social Studies, Science*
Thinking and Learning Activities      48


UNIT III  **ORGANIZATIONAL PATTERN SKILLS**
Overview the Skills      50
*Sequence*
*The 5 W's and Listing*
*Comparison and Contrast; Cause and Effect*

Practice the Skills      53
Applying the Skills in Content Subjects      55
*Language Arts, Social Studies, Science*
Thinking and Learning Activities      74

UNIT IV    **INTERPRETIVE CRITICAL THINKING SKILLS**

Overview the Skills    76
    *Fact or Opinion*
    *Drawing Conclusions*
    *Making Inferences*

Practice the Skills    80
Applying the Skills in Content Subjects    82
    *Language Arts, Social Studies, Science*
Thinking and Learning Activities    102


UNIT V    **HIGHER ORDER CRITICAL THINKING SKILLS**

Overview the Skills    105
    *Reasoning*
    *Theme*
    *Author's Purpose or Bias*

Practice the Skills    108
Applying the Skills in Content Subjects    110
    *Language Arts, Social Studies, Science*
Thinking and Learning Activities    135


UNIT VI    **STUDY SKILLS**

Overview the Skills    138
    *Outlining*
    *Summarizing*
    *Note Taking*

Practice the Skills    142
Applying the Skills in Content Subjects    146
    *Language Arts, Social Studies, Science*
Thinking and Learning Activities    182

# ACKNOWLEDGMENTS

Grateful acknowledgment is made to the following sources for permission to reprint copyrighted materials. Every effort has been made to obtain permission to use previously published material; any errors or omissions are unintentional.

Language Arts Practice B, p. 8. From an article by Sol Feldman appearing in the August 31, 1991, Rochester (NH) *Courier*. Reprinted by permission of the Rochester *Courier*.

Science Practice C, p. 20. From *Environmental Science* (Chiras, 1985). Reprinted by permission of The Benjamin/Cummings Publishing Company.

Social Studies Practice C, p. 40. "Lost Tribes, Lost Knowledge." Copyright 1991 Time Inc. Reprinted by permission.

Language Arts Practice B, p. 57. "Lemond Hopes for a Tour de Force," by Susan Bicklehaupt, 1991. Reprinted courtesy of the Boston *Globe*.

Science Practice A, p. 68. "In Search of the Great White Bear." Copyright 1991 Time Inc. Reprinted by permission.

Language Arts Practice A, p. 82. "Country Music's New Mecca." Copyright 1991 Time Inc. Reprinted by permission.

Language Arts Practice C, p. 87. "Stopping by Woods on a Snowy Evening," by Robert Frost. From THE POETRY OF ROBERT FROST edited by Edward Cannery Latham. Copyright 1923, © 1969 by Henry Holt and Company, Inc. Copyright 1942, 1951 by Robert Frost. Copyright © 1970 by Lesley Frost Ballantine. Reprinted by permission of Henry Holt and Company, Inc.

Social Studies Practice A, p. 89. "Wyoming." Excerpted from *The World Book Encyclopedia*. © 1992 World Book, Inc. By permission of the publisher.

Science Practice C, p. 100. "A New Kind of Kinship," by Joel L. Swerdlow. From *National Geographic*, September 1991. Reprinted by permission.

Language Arts Practice C, p. 116. From "Millie Could Teach the Experts," by Ralph Brauer. Reprinted by permission of Philip G. Spitzer Literary Agency. Copyright © 1989 by Ralph Brauer. Also reprinted with permission from the January 1991 *Reader's Digest*.

Social Studies Practice C, p. 124. From "Check 'Yes;' Improve Campaign Finance System." Copyright 1992, USA TODAY. Reprinted with permission.

Science Practice A, p. 126. Book review by Peter Gorner. © Copyright 1991, Chicago Tribune Company. All rights reserved, used with permission.

Social Studies Practice A, p. 159. "Retracing the First Crusade," by Tim Severin. From *National Geographic*, September 1989. Reprinted by permission.

# Advanced
# Reading Skills

# Unit 1 CONTEXT AND MEANING SKILLS

## Overview the Skills

### 1. FOLLOWING DIRECTIONS

The daily responsibilities at home or at school or at work require you to follow directions to accomplish different tasks.

Sometimes you complete the task with directions that are habit, such as brushing your teeth or operating the dishwasher. Other times you complete the task with formal or written directions, such as tuning up a car or operating a VCR or following a recipe for making a special dessert. For example, the directions for avoiding a fire in the home might be the following:

> To avoid the possibility of a fire in your home, clean junk and unwanted materials out of the attic and basement. Store flammable liquids in proper containers and outside, if possible. Do not overload electric outlets and extension cords.

### On Your Own

Complete the following for making a pizza with the necessary directions in the appropriate order.

1. Stretch the dough into the shape of the pan
2. Spread the sauce evenly over the dough
3. *add cheese over sauce*
4. *include other toppings*
5. *bake for 30 min.*

### 2. VOCABULARY THROUGH CONTEXT CLUES

How to figure out unknown meanings of new words in sentences, without a dictionary, can be a challenging task. Often there are other words in a sentence to help you unlock and understand these new words. These other words are called *context clues*. The skill of using context clues to learn new meanings can save time and trouble. With over 500,000 words in the English language, you cannot look up every new word in the dictionary.

For example, study the following two different sentences and the boldface word in each sentence. Then study the words in italics that are context clues for finding the definition of the boldface word. What is your definition of each new word?

1. Some *people* are **ingrates** because *no matter how much you do* for them or *give them*, they are *never satisfied*.

2. The *price* of *fruits* and *vegetables* often **fluctuates** due to the *unpredictable weather, changing shipping costs,* and *other market conditions.*

**ingrates** _People who Want more than they need_

**fluctuates** _rises or falls_

## On Your Own

Read the following paragraph and notice the boldface words. Find context clues for these words and write the meaning for each.

**Contagious** diseases are easily **transmitted**, or spread, from person to person. Some are transmitted by coughs or sneezes as **droplets** of microscopic mucus are sprayed through the air. These are **inhaled** without realizing it at the time, but later the result can be days of cold or flu suffering.

**contagious** _can easily be given to another person_

**transmitted** _a deasise is in another host,_

**droplets** _a small amount of mucus_

**inhaled** _breathing in._

## 3. LOCATING FACTS AND ANSWERS

One way to better understand what you read is to find facts and information to answer specific questions. These sources of information are the sentences and paragraphs in encyclopedias, textbooks, novels, newspapers, and any other form of printed material.

For example, read the following paragraph and answer the questions about it.

Earthquakes can cause destruction and death. These tremors are felt immediately and cause buildings and roads and other structures to shake or collapse. Severe earthquakes bring death, mostly from falling objects, debris, and fires from broken gas lines.

*1.* What kinds of damage can earthquakes cause?
*2.* What are some of the causes of death from earthquakes?

## On Your Own

Read the following paragraph and then answer the questions that follow by locating information in the paragraph to support your answers.

*The World Almanac* is a vast collection of facts and information about almost any topic that comes to mind, from accidents to zinc production for the year. This annual tome of world data was first published in 1868 and is about a thousand pages of specific insight into people and places, nations and languages, area and zip codes, science and social security, and sports and superstars. These are just a very, very few of the list of topics that will keep you up late at night perusing this quantity of information.

*1.* What is the name of the book from the first sentence?
   The World Almanac

*2.* When was this book first published?
   1868

*3.* List five topics for which you would find information in this book.
   nations
   zip codes
   science

## 4. SENTENCE MEANING

The English language is spoken and written in groups of words that form a complete thought. These complete thoughts are called sentences. Often, sentences are grouped to form paragraphs and paragraphs are grouped to become compositions or stories or articles.

Each sentence has its own meaning and also will add to the meaning of a paragraph when sentences are grouped into a paragraph. Understanding the meaning of a sentence requires you to read and think about the entire sentence, not just individual words or phrases.

For example, you know that sentence 1, below, is about a vacation. What is the meaning of sentence 2?

1. Two weeks at the beach was a welcome rest from school and work for the Alera family.

2. The nervous student fretted as the teacher approached her with first-semester grades in hand.

Notice how the sentence is not just about the student or the teacher or the grades, but the uncertainty and nervousness over all three.

## On Your Own

Read the following sentence and think about its meaning. Then answer the questions that follow.

The field of biology offers career opportunities in botany, zoology, oceanography, and ecology, to name a few, for students who enjoy and excel in this subject at school.

*1.* What word in the entire sentence best tells the meaning of the whole sentence?

<u>biology</u>

2. Rewrite the sentence into a shorter version without changing the overall meaning.

<u>biology has many opportunities where students can enjoy it at school.</u>

## Practice the Skills

**PREREADING**   Natural disasters can occur at any time. Have you properly prepared for such emergencies?

There are many precautions to take to prepare for a natural disaster. However, not much can be done during a hurricane, tornado, flood, earthquake, or severe winter blizzard. Therefore, it is the aftermath of these natural forces that receives the most attention and requires certain directions and guidelines to be followed.

Keep listening to the radio or watching television for updates on local conditions. If you must go outside, check for fallen or damaged power lines and avoid these extreme dangers to your life. Check for leaking gas lines by smelling for any gassy odor. Do not drive unless absolutely necessary. Notify relatives nearby of your condition and check for their concerns or needs. If any serious emergencies requiring medical attention exist, contact organizations such as the Red Cross to assist you. If electricity is lost for extended periods, use flashlights to avoid fire dangers from candles or lanterns.

The list of directions for the period following a major weather disaster could go on, but these serve as a guide. Most often, it is good old-fashioned common sense, along with a little planning, that prevails in times of danger.

## Following Directions

1. For which of the following does the selection give directions for consideration? (*a*) destruction and rescue conditions  (*b*) securing emergency services during a natural disaster  (*c*) developments before a natural disaster  (*d*) procedures to follow after a natural disaster

2. According to the selection, fallen or damaged power lines cause the most danger to  (*a*) television and radio reception  (*b*) human life  (*c*) driving the car (*d*) contacting relatives.

3. Copy the direction that refers specifically to the problem of fire.
   Use flash lights to avoid fire dangers from candles or lanters.

4. How should you check for leaking gas lines according to the selection?  (*a*) by smelling  (*b*) by listening  (*c*) by looking  (*d*) by feeling

## Vocabulary Through Context Clues

5. According to the selection, the word "directions" would be the best context clue for the meaning of which word?  (*a*) attention  (*b*) forces  (*c*) guidelines (*d*) planning

6. What does the word "updates" best refer to in the selection?  (*a*) destruction and rescue conditions  (*b*) natural disasters and rescue teams  (*c*) fires and flashlights (*d*) family and relatives

## Locating Facts and Answers

7. Which sentence in the first paragraph refers to specific types of natural weather disasters?  (*a*) 1st  (*b*) 2nd  (*c*) 3rd  (*d*) all three

8. What organization is specifically referred to in the selection?
   Red cross

## Sentence Meaning

9. The last sentence of the first paragraph refers to what period of time in following directions for natural disasters?  (*a*) before  (*b*) during  (*c*) after  (*d*) none of these

---

10. Rewrite the last sentence of the selection into a new sentence in your own words.

---

---

# Applying the Skills in Content Subjects

## LANGUAGE ARTS PRACTICE A

**PREREADING**   Know the rules of the road and apply those rules to all driving experiences, especially involving a motorcycle.

Good driving habits often make the difference between life and death on the roads and highways of America. This is especially true when driving a motorcycle or carrying a passenger on a motorcycle.

Beginning drivers should practice their skills on a motorcycle during the daylight in areas such as empty parking lots or seldom-used back roads. When driving on regularly traveled roads, allow extra distance from the vehicle in front. This is necessary because of the instability of a motorcycle during a sudden stop. Don't drive between two lanes of traffic; also allow plenty of distance ahead when passing another vehicle. All cycle operators must ride no more than two abreast and maintain single file while passing as a group. Avoid sharp turns; decelerate on slippery roads caused by rain, fog, mud, and sand. Engage both front and rear brakes together when stopping at any time, especially on slippery roads. Above all else, wear protective headgear and some type of face and eye protection to alleviate the possibility of serious injury.

## Following Directions

1. Beginning motorcycle drivers should consider which of the following directions, according to the selection?  (*a*) practice during the evening  (*b*) practice on busy roads  (*c*) practice on weekends  (*d*) practice during the daylight

---

2. A proper procedure for passing another vehicle while driving a motorcycle is the following.  (*a*) travel between two lanes of traffic  (*b*) allow plenty of distance  (*c*) pass two abreast  (*d*) none of these

---

3. Which of the following directions is NOT recommended on slippery roads?
   (*a*) ride sidesaddle   (*b*) engage both brakes   (*c*) decelerate   (*d*) avoid sharp turns

   _____

4. Copy the rule or direction from the selection that refers to equipment to prevent injury while motorcycle driving and riding.

   _____

   _____

   _____

## Vocabulary Through Context Clues

5. The word "decelerate" as used in the selection has a meaning of   (*a*) speed up
   (*b*) slow down   (*c*) maintain speed   (*d*) stop.

   _____

6. Give a definition of your own for the word "alleviate" as used in the selection. Note any context clues.

   _____

## Locating Facts and Answers

7. Which two sentences in the second paragraph refer to directions for passing another vehicle while driving a motorcycle?   (*a*) 1, 3   (*b*) 2, 4   (*c*) 3, 5
   (*d*) 4, 5

   _____

8. Locate and write the two weather words from the selection.

   _____

## Sentence Meaning

9. Rewrite the first sentence of the selection into a new sentence of your own with a similar meaning.

   _____

   _____

10. The last sentence in the selection is about   (*a*) passengers   (*b*) safety   (*c*) braking
    (*d*) weather.

    _____

## LANGUAGE ARTS PRACTICE B

**PREREADING**   Americans love their sports. But which sport is the most exciting for the spectator and dangerous for the athlete?

Oh, to lead the life of a professional athlete! A life of glamour, glitter, and riches—that is, if your athletic abilities are channeled into a sport like baseball, golf, or tennis. But there are thousands of professional athletes who choose to earn a livelihood performing sporting feats that are not only devoid of much glamour but which are downright dangerous. They are the men and the women who compete on the professional rodeo circuit such as the Double R World Championship Rodeo that recently came to Chandler Field at Attitash Mountain in New Hampshire.

Among the athletes attracted by the $20,000 in prize money was a tall, lean young man from Bellaire, Ohio, with the name of Bob Montagne. Montagne's chosen rodeo specialty is the one voted "the most dangerous sporting event in America" by the Sports Writers of America—bull riding.

As he speaks, Montagne is busily preparing to try to earn a paycheck by climbing on the back of a 2,000-pound Brahman bull and staying there for a minimum of eight seconds while the animal bucks, kicks, spins—does everything in its power to dislodge the rider atop its back. If his skills are intact and Lady Luck is riding with him this day, Montagne's efforts could earn him $800. At worst he will end up in the hospital, or perhaps even dead because of injuries from the hooves and horns of the ill-tempered animal.

## *Vocabulary Through Context Clues*

*1.* How would you characterize the definitions of "glamour, glitter, and riches" as used in the selection?   (*a*) mostly alike   (*b*) mostly opposite   (*c*) two are alike   (*d*) two are opposite

_____

*2.* The word "devoid" as used in the selection means   (*a*) full   (*b*) empty   (*c*) creating   (*d*) competing.

_____

*3.* Which word from the selection is closest in meaning to the word "feat" as used in the selection?   (*a*) occasion   (*b*) circuit   (*c*) skills   (*d*) specialty

_____

*4.* Write a sentence of your own using the word "dislodge."

_____

_____

_____

## *Locating Facts and Answers*

**5.** Which sentence in the first paragraph refers to places?  (*a*) 1st  (*b*) 2nd  (*c*) 3rd  (*d*) 4th

_____

**6.** What words from the selection describe what a bull does while being ridden?

_____

_____

**7.** What two parts of the bull can do the most damage to the rider according to the selection?

_____

_____

## *Sentence Meaning*

**8.** The first sentence of the second paragraph is mostly about  (*a*) bull riding  (*b*) Ohio  (*c*) Bob Montagne  (*d*) money.

_____

**9.** Copy the sentence from the selection that means about the same as the following sentence. "If the ride goes his way, Bob could make some money."

_____

_____

_____

**10.** Who or what is "Lady Luck" as used in the selection?

_____

_____

## LANGUAGE ARTS PRACTICE C

**PREREADING**   Driving under the influence of alcohol causes thousands of accidents and deaths each year.

Beginning in kindergarten, continuing throughout grade school, and now one month from graduation, Diane and Celia and Marita were inseparable companions. On this warm May evening with stars stapled into a crescent moon sky, the trio headed to the surf with Celia at the wheel. The route was etched into her memory like the steps in a line dance at a wedding.

One mile ahead, at thirty miles an hour over the posted limit of forty-five, approached a vehicle careening toward chaos. The traveling timebomb drifted aimlessly left of center, right of center, and left of center with consistent accuracy. The mind is a misguided focus on double yellow lines when one hand is on a wheel and the other around a bottle. With an expression of indifference to task, a radio at maximum decibel level, and tires screaming for relief, the driver threw responsibility to the wind.

As distance between the two evaporated to a very precious few feet, reaction time to escaping fate ticked to an end. Like a breath across a flickering candle, four lives skidded to a premature halt. Four lives were embalmed into eternity. Four potentially wonderful contributions to a better world were denied such opportunity.

## Vocabulary Through Context Clues

1. Which of the following would be a synonym for the word "careening" as used in the selection?   (*a*) escaping   (*b*) hurtling   (*c*) denying   (*d*) throwing

_____

2. Give two or three context clue words and a definition for the word "decibel" as used in the selection.

_____

_____

_____

3. Give a definition of your own for the word "evaporated" as used in the selection.

_____

_____

4. The word "precious" as used in the selection means   (*a*) endless   (*b*) important   (*c*) expensive   (*d*) none of these.

_____

_____

## Locating Facts and Answers

5. Copy two phrases that refer to the weather in the selection.

_____

_____

6. Which sentence in the first paragraph tells you that the girls had been to the surf before?   (*a*) 1st   (*b*) 2nd   (*c*) 3rd   (*d*) all three

_____

7. Copy two words or phrases from the selection that mean "car."

_____

_____

## Sentence Meaning

**8.** Rewrite the first sentence of the second paragraph into a new sentence of your own with the same meaning.

_____

_____

_____

**9.** Explain what is happening in the last sentence of the second paragraph.

_____

_____

_____

**10.** Which sentence in the last paragraph first tells of death? (*a*) 1st (*b*) 2nd (*c*) 3rd (*d*) 4th

_____

## SOCIAL STUDIES PRACTICE A

**PREREADING** Have you ever thought about running for public office? Assuming a candidacy is a major responsibility.

Democracy means government by the people. Thus, we enjoy the right to run for public office as a candidate, and the right to vote for candidates. Deciding to run for office and planning a campaign for election usually involves much time and expense.

The following ten directions may help to organize a campaign and to understand how this aspect of the democratic process works.

1. Visit your local town hall and take out nomination papers for the office that you plan to seek.
2. Check the deadline date for returning these papers, which require a certain number of signatures. These signatures must be by registered voters who live within the district boundaries that you will represent.
3. Announce your candidacy in the local newspapers with some interesting notes about your background and reasons for running. At the same time, begin to establish a campaign organization of family, friends, and neighbors.
4. Formulate a platform of ideas, issues, and plans that are of interest to the voters and important to the town or district. This platform must separate you from other candidates and generate interest for the citizens to vote for you.
5. Schedule fund-raisers such as dances, socials, informal parties, barbecues, and breakfasts. Raising money and financing a campaign are major concerns for any serious candidacy.

6. Decide how the platform will be delivered to the voters. Options are television, radio, newspaper ads, brochures or flyers, and the traditional door-to-door meeting with the voters.
7. Print bumper stickers and signs and buttons and any other campaign paraphernalia to get your name on the streets.
8. Attend as many community meetings as possible so that concerned citizens will know that you are a serious and interested candidate.
9. Hold regular meetings with the people who are in your organization to get input and strategy, and also to keep momentum to election day.
10. Get your people out on election day, be personally visible to as many voters as possible, and plan a party on election night (win or lose) to thank all who gave their support.

## Following Directions

*1.* The ten directions given in the selection explain how to   (*a*) interview for a public job   (*b*) run for public office   (*c*) raise money for charity   (*d*) write campaign stories.

_____

*2.* Which of the following is NOT related to "nomination papers" according to the selection?   (*a*) money   (*b*) signatures   (*c*) deadline dates   (*d*) town hall

_____

*3.* Name three things that should be printed to get people to recognize your name during a campaign.

_____

_____

_____

*4.* What do the directions specifically instruct a candidate to attend?

_____

_____

## Vocabulary Through Context Clues

*5.* Which of the following is NOT a context clue for the meaning of "democracy" as used in the selection?   (*a*) the right to run for public office   (*b*) the right to vote for candidates   (*c*) collecting money for campaigns   (*d*) government by the people

_____

*6.* The word "platform" as used in the selection means   (*a*) ideas   (*b*) speaking area   (*c*) supporters   (*d*) fund-raisers.

_____

## Locating Facts and Answers

*7.* What numbered direction specifically discusses money?

_____

*8.* What numbered direction answers "what to do on election day"?

_____

## Sentence Meaning

*9.* Which two direction numbers are mostly about people?　(*a*) 1, 3　(*b*) 4,5
(*c*) 3, 9　(*d*) 6, 10

_____

*10.* Rewrite direction #9 into your own words.

_____

_____

_____

## SOCIAL STUDIES PRACTICE B

**PREREADING**　Every four years a presidential inauguration ceremony is held in Washington, D.C. Some inaugurations have become memorable in American history.

Jan. 20, 1961. Over half a foot of pristine snow blanketed Washington last night, leaving the air this morning bitterly cold and pure. Some 20,000 people in coats and scarves massed before the East Portico of the Capitol, prepared for the swearing-in of the nation's 35th President. They expected the typical inauguration speech of rehearsed guarantees and praise for the constituency. John F. Kennedy, however, promised nothing and demanded everything.

"In your hands, my fellow citizens, more than mine, will rest the final success or failure of our course," Kennedy said. "Now the trumpet summons us again . . . against the common enemies of man: tyranny, poverty, disease, and war itself." In the war against war, Kennedy intimated he was ready to negotiate with the Soviets on the inspection and control of nuclear arms. He praised NATO and the U.N. for their peace-keeping efforts.

"The torch has been passed to a new generation of Americans," he said. Some listeners imagined he compared himself to the departing Eisenhower, nearly a generation older than he. But Kennedy meant more. "And so, my fellow Americans," he said, "ask not what your country can do for you—ask what you can do for your country."

## Vocabulary Through Context Clues

**1.** Using the context clues in the sentence, the best definition for "massed" would be  (*a*) assembled  (*b*) dispersed  (*c*) froze  (*d*) spoke.

---

**2.** The word *constituency* most likely refers to  (*a*) places  (*b*) ideas  (*c*) president  (*d*) people.

---

**3.** The best definition for the word "intimated" is  (*a*) held back  (*b*) hinted  (*c*) denied  (*d*) praised.

---

**4.** Write a sentence of your own using the word "negotiate" with a comparable meaning to its definition in the selection.

---

---

---

## Locating Facts and Answers

**5.** In numerical order, which President of the United States was John F. Kennedy?

---

**6.** Which of the following is NOT one of the "common enemies of man" in the selection?  (*a*) NATO  (*b*) poverty  (*c*) tyranny  (*d*) war

---

**7.** Which paragraph contains the specific name of another person?  (*a*) 1st  (*b*) 2nd  (*c*) 3rd  (*d*) none of them

---

## Sentence Meaning

**8.** Which sentence in the first paragraph is not about people?  (*a*) 1st  (*b*) 2nd  (*c*) 3rd  (*d*) 4th

---

**9.** Rewrite the following into your own words. "Now the trumpet summons us again . . . against the common enemies of man:"

---

---

---

**10.** The first sentence of the last paragraph is about a  (*a*) war  (*b*) fire  (*c*) responsibility  (*d*) disease.

---

## SOCIAL STUDIES PRACTICE C

**PREREADING**   It is necessary to study the past in order to understand the present and plan for the future. History provides such an opportunity.

Throughout the past several centuries of developing western European civilizations, it was the agrarian or farming society that formed social and economic progress. Even in the settlement and expansion of America in the 1600's–1800's, the farming society was the norm until the turn of the 20th century. This time in American history, beginning about two centuries ago, is known as the industrial revolution. It meant the emergence of industry and factories. It also meant the birth and growth of cities, called urbanization.

The shift from the farming society to the industrial society was the shift from independent and rural living to a system of dependent and urban living, earning wages from an employer. It also provided for beginning one's own business. This flourishing of business with wages and profits and employers and employees became the basis of what we know as capitalism, the whole foundation of our present economic system. Capitalism is the right to free enterprise, the market economy of open trade within America and the world, the right to earn a living through any legal trade or product.

The explosion of technological advancement after World War II initiated the present shift from the industrial society to what we refer to as the information society and service economy of America. Fewer Americans work in factories, and even fewer work on farms. As we begin the 21st century, what looms as the next society for America as we study the shift from wood chips to microchips?

## *Vocabulary Through Context Clues*

1. Copy the context clues that direct you to the meaning of the word "agrarian."
   _farming society_

2. The word "norm" as used in the selection means   (*a*) change   (*b*) product   (*c*) custom   (*d*) right.
   C

3. Which of the following is NOT a part of the definition of "capitalism" as the word is used in the selection?   (*a*) open trade   (*b*) free enterprise   (*c*) market economy   (*d*) America in the 1600's–1800's
   d

4. Using the context clues for the word "looms," what time frame exists?   (*a*) past   (*b*) present   (*c*) future   (*d*) all three
   c

## *Locating Facts and Answers*

5. Copy the two sentences that define the "industrial revolution."

   *the explotion of technology after WWll.*

6. Locate and copy three phrases in the second paragraph that describe or refer to the "industrial society."

   *the shift from indipendant to rural living, the flourishing of buisness dependant, emploryees.*

7. Which sentence in the last paragraph discusses where Americans now do not work?  (*a*) 1st  (*b*) 2nd  (*c*) 3rd  (*d*) all three

   *a*

## *Sentence Meaning*

8. Rewrite the first sentence of the selection into a new sentence in your own words.

   *Europes developement throughout the centuries has been increasing*

9. The "shift" that is referred to in the first sentence of the second paragraph is a shift from  (*a*) independent to rural living  (*b*) rural living to earned wages from an employer  (*c*) earned wages to one's own business  (*d*) none of these.

10. The "shift" that is referred to in the first sentence of the last paragraph is a shift from  (*a*) farms to factories  (*b*) World War I to World War II  (*c*) information to service economy  (*d*) industrial society to information society.

### SCIENCE PRACTICE A

**PREREADING**   America must become more aware of the environment through such programs as recycling. Often, awareness is developed through practicing good habits.

Recycling is here to stay. The average American home discards tons of trash on an annual basis. This volume of rubbish simply cannot be contained in the overused landfills of rural and suburban areas or burned in the expensive industrial incinerator plants of urban America. A household recycling program must become a regular habit.

Separate recyclable materials such as paper, glass, cans, and plastic from other household garbage. Obtain containers with appropriate labels or use bins provided by the town for storage of recyclables until collection day or for deposit at local collection sites.

Separate paper products such as newspapers, magazines, and cardboard into three piles. All cans must be separated into aluminum or tin and both types should be washed and kept from insects. Glass bottles that contained food or drink products need to be sorted according to color—clear, brown, or green. Mirrors and light bulbs, for example, are not recyclable materials. Plastic containers of soft drink and milk products should be compacted or squashed and the caps discarded. (NOTE: Some states require deposits on aluminum cans and plastic and glass bottles for drink products to insure recycling.)

Contact local landfills or town departments for the appropriate disposal of hazardous waste products. These would include pesticides, oil-base paints, wood stains, acids, poisons, certain cleaning products, car oil, and car batteries. These products must be sealed and NEVER disposed of with household trash or flushed into water systems. Also, store these lethal materials outside, if possible, while awaiting proper disposal.

## Following Directions

1. How should paper products be separated, according to the recycling directions?

_____

_____

2. Which direction applies to tin or aluminum cans?  (*a*) keep from insects  (*b*) store with glass  (*c*) do not wash  (*d*) discard caps

_____

3. What two examples of glass products in the selection are not recyclable?

_____

4. Which of the following directions regarding hazardous waste products is NOT mentioned in the selection?  (*a*) must be sealed  (*b*) never flush into water systems  (*c*) store outside  (*d*) store with paper products

_____

## Vocabulary Through Context Clues

5. The words "rural," "suburban," and "urban" as used in the selection refer to  (*a*) people  (*b*) places  (*c*) business  (*d*) materials.

_____

6. What word in the selection serves as both a context clue and a definition for the word "compacted"?

_____

## Locating Facts and Answers

7. Which sentence in the first paragraph answers the question, "How much trash is discarded by American homes?"  (*a*) 1st  (*b*) 2nd  (*c*) 3rd  (*d*) 4th

_____

**8.** Copy the sentence that contains the examples of hazardous waste products.

_____

_____

_____

_____

## Sentence Meaning

**9.** Which two sentences in the first paragraph have almost the same meaning? (*a*) 1, 2  (*b*) 2, 3  (*c*) 1, 4  (*d*) 2, 4

_____

**10.** Copy the sentence from the selection that means the same as the following made-up sentence. "These products should be cleaned and stored away from bugs."

_____

_____

_____

## SCIENCE PRACTICE B

**PREREADING**   The natural wonders of the universe never cease to be amazing. Consider the spectacular display of the full solar eclipse.

Mother Nature provides many spectacular events, but none may be more intriguing and mystifying than a full solar eclipse. This event is the rare merging of time and place as the moon passes across the face of the sun and blocks its light. The most memorable views can be found at high altitudes during clear daylight. Previous travel planning may be necessary.

This several minute cosmic phenomenon dazzles all viewers, amateur and professional, who behold the vista for a variety of reasons. As daylight dissolves into darkness, the moon becomes a drawn window shade. The solar prominences form the corona of pearly white flashes with pink accents. These flaring gasses explode off the sun's surface while scientists search for information about the sun's structure. The data collected will assist in revising theories about how the sun and other stars are made. How the universe originated is the big question that scientists ponder, discuss, and hopefully decide someday with final proof.

In the meantime, it is the simple natural occurrence of the eclipse that draws attention. It is the time when Mother Nature gives us a nudge and reminds us to behold the wonders in space. It may unlock the questions of science someday, but in the present the solar eclipse jogs the memory and reduces us to simple mortals.

## *Vocabulary Through Context Clues*

1. Using context clues, would you say that the definition of "intriguing" is
   (*a*) boring  (*b*) important  (*c*) fascinating  (*d*) mystifying.

   _____

2. Which of the following words relates most to the word "prominences"?  (*a*) data
   (*b*) corona  (*c*) mortals  (*d*) orbit

   _____

3. Rewrite the sentence containing the word "data" by replacing "data" with a word
   of your own and keeping the sentence meaning the same.

   _____

   _____

   _____

4. Think about the meaning of the word "ponder" as used in the selection. You
   would most likely "ponder" (*a*) a space  (*b*) a nudge  (*c*) a proof  (*d*) a problem.

   _____

## *Locating Facts and Answers*

5. The definition of an eclipse is given in which sentence of the first paragraph?
   (*a*) 1st  (*b*) 2nd  (*c*) 3rd  (*d*) 4th

   _____

6. About how long does an eclipse last from beginning to end?

   _____

7. Copy the sentence from the selection that answers the following question. "What
   colors are coronas?"

   _____

   _____

   _____

## *Sentence Meaning*

8. Rewrite the second sentence of the second paragraph into another sentence in
   your own words.

   _____

   _____

9. How many other complete sentences in the selection relate to the reason why
   "scientists search for information during an eclipse"?  (*a*) 1  (*b*) 2  (*c*) 3
   (*d*) none

   _____

**10.** How many sentences in the last paragraph relate to "time"?  (**a**) 1  (**b**) 2  (**c**) 3 (**d**) none of them

---

## SCIENCE PRACTICE C

**PREREADING**   Protecting water supplies from pollution is a responsibility for every country on earth. Otherwise, future generations will suffer the consequences.

Water pollution is any physical or chemical change in water that can adversely affect organisms. It is a global problem, affecting both the industrialized and the developing nations. The water pollution problems in the rich and the poor nations, however, are quite different in many respects. Heat, toxic or poisonous metals, acids, sediment, animal and human wastes, and synthetic organic compounds foul the waterways of developed nations. Human and animal wastes, sediment, and pathogenic organisms head the list in the nonindustrialized nations. In these countries, unsanitary water and malnutrition account for most of the illness and death.

Water has many different uses, each requiring different levels of purity. For example, water from the Ohio River may be clean enough to wash steel but may be toxic to fish and wildlife. Ohio water suitable for boating or fishing may be unsuitable for swimming. This river water, safe to swim in, may be too polluted to drink.

Like air pollutants, water pollutants come from numerous natural and anthropogenic (man-made) sources. Likewise, water pollutants produced in one nation may flow into others, creating complex international control problems that may take decades to solve.*

## *Vocabulary Through Context Clues*

**1.** Any physical or chemical change in water that can adversely affect organisms is called  (**a**) malnutrition  (**b**) developing nations  (**c**) water pollution  (**d**) synthetic organic compounds.

c

---

**2.** Using context clues, give a short definition of your own for the word "global" as used in the selection.

all over the world

---

**3.** The word "foul" as used in the selection means  (**a**) improve  (**b**) pollute (**c**) develop  (**d**) decrease.

b

---

*From *Environmental Science* (Chiras; 1985). Reprinted by permission of The Benjamin/Cummings Publishing Company.

**4.** The word "toxic" as used in the selection means   (***a***) safe   (***b***) wasteful
   (***c***) available   (***d***) dangerous.

*d*

## Locating Facts and Answers

**5.** What two things account for most of the illness and death in nonindustrialized
   nations, according to the selection?

*Water pollution, malnutrition*

**6.** Which of the following is mentioned in the selection as a use for water from the
   Ohio River?   (***a***) washing steel   (***b***) feeding animals   (***c***) electric power
   (***d***) growing crops

*a*

**7.** Which paragraph contains the most facts related to the specific causes of pollution?
   (***a***) 1   (***b***) 2   (***c***) 3   (***d***) all three are about the same

## Sentence Meaning

**8.** Copy the sentence from the selection that means about the same as the following
   sentence. "There are many differences between the pollution problems of developed and undeveloped nations."

*Likewise water pollutants produced in one nation may flow into others.*

**9.** What is meant by the phrase "different levels of purity" as used in the selection?

*things are cleaner than others.*

**10.** Which sentence(s) in the last paragraph refer to both air and water pollutants?
   (***a***) 1   (***b***) 2   (***c***) both   (***d***) neither

## Thinking and Learning Activities
*Complete independently or in cooperative groups*

### WITHIN A SELECTION (SEE SCIENCE PRACTICE C)

**1.  Know**   List the five most difficult vocabulary words from the selection and write
a definition for each, using the dictionary.

**2.  Comprehend**   Locate what you think is the most difficult sentence in the selection
and rewrite it into a new sentence of your own without changing the meaning.

**3. Apply**   Use the facts and information from the selection to answer three of your own original questions. Write the questions and the answers in complete sentences.

**4. Analyze**   Group the pollution problems of rich nations in a column A and the pollution problems of poor nations in a column B.

**5. Synthesize**   Arrange the uses of water from the Ohio River from what you think are the most important to the least important in numerical order.

**6. Evaluate**   Select what you think is the most important sentence in the selection and give two reasons for your choice. Use complete sentences.

## BEYOND A SELECTION (SEE LANGUAGE ARTS PRACTICE B)

**1. Know**   Name five other sports that you think are as dangerous as bull riding.

**2. Comprehend**   Describe one account of one of these sports from a newspaper or magazine article in a few sentences of your own. Use vocabulary words associated with the danger and the sport.

**3. Apply**   Illustrate a scene of danger from one of these five sports. Use pictures or drawings of your own.

**4. Analyze**   Examine one of these sports closely and write three directions for avoiding injury while participating in this sport.

**5. Synthesize**   Design a list of the five most serious injuries that you think are associated with one of these sports.

**6. Evaluate**   Estimate the medical bill for one of the five injuries with specific dollar facts and information.

## ABOUT A SELECTION (SEE SOCIAL STUDIES PRACTICE B)

Use primary and secondary reference material about John F. Kennedy to compile facts and information about his life and presidency. Complete a report of several paragraphs with 4–7 sentences in each paragraph.

In the first few paragraphs, explain his life before becoming President. In the next few paragraphs, explain the problems and accomplishments while he was President. In the final few paragraphs, explain how his presidency still affects our country today.

# Unit II TECHNICAL COMPREHENSION SKILLS

## Overview the Skills

### 1. MAJOR AND MINOR TOPICS

When you read, notice that the author often presents topics in a certain structure. In one kind of structure, *major* topic means "general" and *minor* topic means "specific."

Think about the appliances in the average home. Examples would be washing machine, microwave, disposal, and refrigerator. Let's put this information into the following paragraph:

> The average American home has many appliances, such as the washing machine, the microwave oven, and the sink disposal. The refrigerator is also a very necessary appliance. All of these help in the daily routine.

Now think about the general *major* topic of "appliances in the home" and the specific *minor* topics of "washing machine, microwave oven, sink disposal, refrigerator." Take a look at this example and the answers in chart form:

Major Topic:   Appliances in the home

Minor Topics:
1. washing machine
2. microwave oven
3. sink disposal
4. refrigerator

### On Your Own

Complete the following with information of your own.

Major Topic:   Activities to join at school or at work

Minor Topics:
1. _____Dogbe ball_____
2. _____kick ball_____
3. _____ultamite Frisbee_____
4. _____

## 2. MAIN IDEA AND TOPIC SENTENCE

Finding the main idea means finding or understanding what the whole paragraph or selection is about, either in a few words of your own or one sentence from the written material.

To understand the main idea completely, you must also understand how a good paragraph is structured. Most paragraphs contain the following components:

1. Topic Sentence: introduces the main topic; it is usually the first sentence, but sometimes it is the last.
2. Supporting Sentences: explain, expand, or give examples of the main topic.
3. Concluding Sentence: finishes or sums up the main topic and is the last sentence.

The key to understanding the main idea is to study the topic sentence and the supporting sentences to come up with a short statement about all of the information. For example, notice the following three-sentence paragraph that follows the structure for a good paragraph:

> Most students have used a public library for one reason or another. The library offers a place to study or complete reports, borrow books for leisure reading, or gather research information for term papers. This valuable community asset serves the entire population of a city or town.

You know from reading the topic sentence and the following two that the main idea is about the library. But, what about the library? Is the main idea about building a library, the cost of a library, or the use of a library? Explain your answer. Can you make up a title for this paragraph? Titles are often parts of the main idea.

### On Your Own

Read the following paragraph and answer the questions that follow:

> College football has become big business in America. Each Saturday during the fall and into New Year's Day with the bowl games, the nation's airwaves are flooded with football programming from around the country. Stadium capacities are approaching 100,000 spectators for panoramic views of the gridiron match-ups on all television networks. The advertising costs to sponsors and the profits to television are well into the millions of dollars. One viewing of a major college football game will quickly give the scope of just how big college football has become.

*1.* The main idea is about   (*a*) professional football   (*b*) sports   (*c*) college football   (*d*) education.

2. Which of the following about the main idea is most important?   (*a*) attendance (*b*) players   (*c*) holidays   (*d*) matchups

---

3. Copy the topic sentence from the selection.

---

---

4. Write a title for the selection.

---

## 3. DETAILS

Everything that you read or listen to or observe or experience is filled with details. Details are specific bits of information that add color and meaning to people, places, things, ideas, emotions, and feelings. Details also often appeal to the senses of sight, sound, touch, taste, and smell. Details give information and enrich meaning. The effective use of details makes your reading more enjoyable and your writing more meaningful.

For example, read the following two sentences that lack details:

The detective entered the basement for a final look.

Cindy was worried as the interview for the debate team was minutes away.

Now read the same two sentences with colorful and meaningful details:

The weary detective tramped into the dark and musty basement for one final search for a shred of evidence.

Usually the walking example of composure, Cindy counted the seconds with sweaty palms clenched as the interview for the debate team was about to commence.

### On Your Own

Add details in the spaces provided for the first sentence and then rewrite the second sentence with as many good details as possible to make it more meaningful.

*1.* The _____ air snapped at Marshall's _____

as the rock-climbing team slowly and _____ advanced up the

steep and _____ face of the mountain.

*2.* The girls practiced every day for the big doubles tennis match on Saturday.

_____

_____

# 4. SIGNAL WORDS

English has over a half million words, but you must look for just a few called *signal words* when reading. These signal words are often used to change meaning (or add meaning or highlight meaning). These words are meaning-change signals. The two most common forms of signal words are adverbs and conjunctions. Notice the following categories of signal words and examples for each.

## A. Adverb Signal Words

**1. Answers "Where?"**  here, there, forward, backward, up, down, by, behind, nearby, around
> Jason patiently stood *behind* the elderly man, while the crowd surged *forward* to the ticket window.

**2. Answers "When?"**  now, ever, never, finally, then, later, always, immediately, recently, first, second, third, daily, today, whenever
> The friendship of Sandra and Sonja just *recently* seemed to be falling apart *whenever* they met, but other friends *immediately* intervened to talk over concerns.

**3. Answers "How?"**  well, rather, very, forcefully, surprisingly, amazingly, fortunately, childishly, fervently, succinctly, perilously, ominously, lovingly
> The battered lacrosse team *fervently* fought throughout the game against a team that was *amazingly* talented with *rather* advanced skills.

## B. Conjunction Signal Words

**1. Adds idea**  and, besides, moreover, or
> Preparing for tests can be done alone *or* in group structure.

**2. Contrasts**  but, however, yet, otherwise, unless
> The Cone Shop did a good ice-cream business, *however,* nothing like the lines at Shibley's around the corner.

**3. Gives pairs of ideas**  either-or, both-and, not only-but also
> *Either* the Democrats *or* the Republicans will stake the right to occupy the White House every four years.

**4. Gives results**  thus, therefore, hence
> All parties were in agreement, *therefore* the contract was signed.

**5. Explains, gives examples**  that is, for example, for instance, such as
> Always demonstrate good table manners in public *such as* proper use of eating utensils, good posture while seated, and a low tone of voice during conversation.

**6. Shows cause or purpose**  because, since, for, in order that
> World order among many countries is changing rapidly *since* the abrupt end of Communist rule in Russia and many European states.

7. **Compares**   like, as
   Tiffany moved through the floor exercises of the competition *like* a polished ballerina in the final act.

## On Your Own

Complete each sentence with adverb and conjunction signal words that make sense. Then write what the signal words do (answers "How?" adds idea, shows cause or purpose, etc.).

*1. a.* _____ the fire trucks arrived, _____ high winds _____ hindered their efforts.

   *b.* What the signal words do: _____

*2. a.* Children are _____ interested in learning, _____ playing _____ eating are _____ their first choices of activity.
   *b.* What the signal words do: _____

# Practice the Skills

**PREREADING**   Good health involves diet, exercise, and proper life-style. When should health awareness begin?

Doctors, health professionals, and teachers are worried about the poor physical fitness of too many young people in America. Studies show that nearly fifty percent of the younger generation exhibit the inability to perform basic fitness tests. Also apparent are test results showing escalating blood pressure, cholesterol, and weight levels. This trend will mean increased heart disease and diabetes. Other disorders are also likely to affect the quality of life in future years.

There are several causes for this decline in physical fitness. First, fewer younger people walk or ride a bike to school or work, and second, less physical education is required or offered in schools and colleges. Third, younger Americans watch an average of 25 hours of television weekly, which is more time than that spent in school or at work. Finally, and most important, America is now the "fast-food society" of poor eating habits with far too much intake of fatty, sugary, and salty foods. These are not nutritious.

A regular aerobic exercise program combining fast walking, cycling, running, or swimming is a good start to improving and maintaining fitness. If you cannot enjoy daily exercise at school, then start a fitness club with friends or join a community health center. Spend a little less time watching television and substitute that time with physical activity. Most important, eat more nutritious foods such as fruits, vegetables, lean meat, and fish. Try to reduce the fatty and sugary and salty foods such as fries, burgers, candy, and soft drinks. A change in the habits of exercise and diet can go a long way toward creating a healthier America into the next century.

## Major and Minor Topics

1. Which of the following are the minor topics for the major topic "medical concerns shown in test results"? (*a*) fat, sugar, salt, (*b*) doctors, health professionals, teachers (*c*) blood pressure, cholesterol, weight (*d*) cycling, running, swimming

2. Give several minor topics from the second paragraph for the major topic "causes or factors in the decline of physical fitness."

3. Which of the following would be a major topic from the selection for the minor topics "fruits, vegetables, lean meat, fish"? (*a*) nonnutritious foods (*b*) nutritious foods (*c*) high-carbohydrate foods (*d*) "fast-food society" foods

## Main Idea and Topic Sentence

4. Which of the following do you think is the best main idea for the selection? (*a*) health and fitness centers are a growing business (*b*) heart disease is a growing concern for doctors (*c*) the fast-food generation needs medical help (*d*) the physical fitness of younger Americans needs attention

5. Copy the sentence from the second paragraph that you think is the topic sentence.

6. The last sentence in the final paragraph is both the concluding and topic sentence for this paragraph. Rewrite it into a new topic sentence and then notice how it could also be the first sentence in this paragraph.

## Details

7. How much time do young Americans spend watching television according to the selection?

*8.* What specific fatty, salty, and sugary foods are mentioned in the selection?

_____

_____

## Signal Words

*9.* What conjunction signal word is used in the following sentence? "This trend will mean increased heart disease and diabetes."

_____

What function does this signal word serve in the sentence?   (*a*) contrasts (*b*) adds   (*c*) compares   (*d*) explains

_____

*10.* In the second to the last sentence of the second paragraph, what are the adverb signal words used to introduce the sentence?

_____

# Applying the Skills in Content Subjects

## LANGUAGE ARTS PRACTICE A

**PREREADING**   When was the last time you won a prize or award? Honors for hard work and significant performance exist throughout all facets of American society.

Throughout the years of growing up and adulthood, the spirit of competition for prizes and awards is often the driving force or motivation to excel. These prizes and rewards are the result of hard work on the athletic fields, at school, or in the workplace. Some awards involve money, but most are meritorious. This means the honor of being recognized as the very best among peers in a particular sport or vocation.

Some of these highest awards for national and world recognition follow. The winter and summer Olympic Games held every four years recognize the first three athletes in each event with gold, silver, and bronze medals. College football credits the best interior lineman with the Outland Award, and the best overall lineman with the Vince Lombardi Award. The best football player in America receives the prestigious Heisman Trophy. Major league baseball in both leagues presents the Most Valuable Player Award, and the Cy Young Award to the best pitcher. Also, the batting champion, the homerun champion, and the Rookie of the Year share the spotlight.

The world of entertainment honors its best performing artists with the Academy Awards for movies, the Tony Awards for plays on stage, the Emmy Awards for television, and the Grammy Awards for recording. The Nobel Prizes are held in the highest esteem by professionals in the fields of literature, sciences, and peace efforts. Categories for the Pulitzer Prizes in journalism include news, photography, sports, and editorials. Also recognized are literary works such as essays, fiction and nonfiction works, and poetry. Pulitzers are also awarded for distinguished musical compositions. These two famous awards were initiated by the contributions of Alfred B. Nobel, who invented dynamite, and Joseph Pulitzer, who was a newspaper publisher in St. Louis and New York. While many, many other awards recognize hard work and ability, all of the honors mentioned in this selection stand out as the most distinguished in national and world recognition.

## *Major/Minor Topics*

1. The major topic for the minor topics "gold, silver, and bronze medals" would be (*a*) Heisman football awards  (*b*) Major League Baseball awards  (*c*) Olympic Games awards  (*d*) World of Entertainment awards.

   _____

2. Which of the following would NOT be a minor topic for the major topic "entertainment honors"?  (*a*) Emmy Award  (*b*) Outland Award  (*c*) Tony Award  (*d*) Grammy Award

   _____

3. List three minor topics from the selection for the major topic "categories for Pulitzer Prizes in journalism."

   _____

   _____

## *Main Idea and Topic Sentence*

4. Which of the following do you think is the best main idea for this selection?  (*a*) there are national and world recognition awards for excellence in sports, entertainment, science, and writing  (*b*) competition for the Heisman and Oscar Awards involves many athletes and actors  (*c*) the Pulitzer Prizes are the most distinguished awards in the world  (*d*) competition is the most important factor in good performance

   _____

5. Make up a good title of your own for this selection.

   _____

6. Which of the three paragraphs in the selection has the topic sentence as the last or concluding sentence?  (*a*) 1st  (*b*) 2nd  (*c*) 3rd  (*d*) all of them

   _____

## Details

7. What is the name of the award given to the best pitcher in each league of major league baseball? (*a*) Vince Lombardi Award (*b*) Heisman Trophy (*c*) Most Valuable Player Award (*d*) Cy Young Award

8. What did Alfred B. Nobel invent?

## Signal Words

9. What signal word as used in the selection tells you that not all awards involve money? (*a*) and (*b*) but (*c*) or (*d*) often

10. What signal word in the selection is used to introduce the fact that there are additional sports awards?

## LANGUAGE ARTS PRACTICE B

**PREREADING** Name the most unique sporting event that you ever observed. Was frog-jumping the answer?

The Calaveras Jumping Frog Jubilee is held in Angels Camp, California, during the third weekend of each May. Calaveras County was the "Mother Lode" of the California gold rush over a century ago. And Angels Camp was the center of things—a wild, rollicking town full of miners seeking gold and, on weekends, any kind of amusement. Frog racing and jumping became popular, and miners waged huge sums of money on contenders. Jim Smiley, a local gambler, was the owner of the best jumper and paraded around town with "Dan'l Webster" in a basket under his arm.

The summer of 1865, Mark Twain rented a nearby cabin and, after witnessing an earlier jubilee, wrote "The Celebrated Jumping Frog of Calaveras County," which became an instant hit from coast to coast.

Not until May of 1928 did the citizens of Angels Camp reenact those early frog jumps to celebrate the paving of their streets. The winning frog that year was "Pride of San Joaquin" (san walk EEN) with a jump of three feet, nine inches. The third weekend of May has been attracting "Amphibian Armadas" ever since.

The rules are pretty simple. All contenders must be at least four inches in length from nose to tail; evidence of drugging will result in disqualification; junior division entry fees are 50 cents per frog, and all other entries are $3 each. Over a two-day period 3,000 to 4,000 frogs will compete in various heats. The prizes are no small peanuts: $1,500 if your frog sets a new world's record during the grand finals, $500 for winning the finals but setting no records. The current record holder is Rosie the Ribiter, who jumped 21 feet, 5 and 3/4 inches in three leaps in 1986.

Frogs come from all over the world, including the world's frog capital, Rayne, Louisiana. For information: International Frog Jump, P.O. Box 96, Angels Camp, CA 95222.

## Major/Minor Topics

1. Three minor topics from the selection for the major topic "what Mark Twain did in the summer of 1865" would be  (*a*) rented a cabin, met Jim Smiley, mined for gold  (*b*) waged sums of money, paraded around town, wrote a story  (*c*) rented a cabin, witnessed a jubilee, wrote a story  (*d*) visited Angels Camp, entered a frog race with Dan'l Webster, won $1500.

2. What would be a major topic from the selection for the minor topics that follow? (*a*) contenders must be four inches in length  (*b*) drugging will result in disqualification  (*c*) junior entry fees are 50 cents  (*d*) all other entries are $3 each

3. What three minor topics from the selection would be listed under the major topic "names of winning frogs at the Calaveras Jubilee"?

   *four inches long, No drugging, and 50 cents a frog*

## Main Idea and Topic Sentence

4. Which of the following topics would be most important in developing a main idea for this selection?  (*a*) Calaveras Jumping Frog Jubilee  (*b*) California gold rush  (*c*) Mark Twain  (*d*) prize amounts

5. Which of the following titles do you think is most appropriate for this selection? (*a*) Frog Training for the Calaveras Jubilee Lasts All Year  (*b*) Animals Break Records Each May in California Contest  (*c*) Angels Camp, California, Becoming Top American Tourist Attraction  (*d*) The Cavaleras Jumping Frog Jubilee Is Part of American History.

6. Copy two of the topic sentences from two different paragraphs in the selection.

   *In 1865 Mark twain rented a cadin after witnessing the Jubalie, not until 1962 did the citizens reanact*

## Details

7. What did Dan'l Webster's owner use to carry him around town?

_____

8. When did Rosie the Ribiter establish the current world record?

_____

## Signal Words

9. What adverb signal words are used in the following sentence? "The third weekend of May has been attracting 'Amphibian Armadas' ever since." What do these words answer?
   (*a*) has been attracting—where   (*b*) ever since—when   (*c*) third weekend—when   (*d*) of May—when

_____

10. What conjunction signal word explains the difference between the $1500 and $500 prizes?

_____

### LANGUAGE ARTS PRACTICE C

**PREREADING**   Understanding the means with which the English language has grown will expand vocabulary. It will also give insight into the future trends of the language.

Imagine looking into a late night 4th of July sky and observing the first fireworks display. Then quickly, shift the imagination to the spectacular conclusion of such a display. The difference between the two can be compared to the growth and changes in the English language during the past 400 years. A language that once contained 25,000 words in the 1500's today numbers over 500,000 and is growing daily. Becoming a linguist or etymologist today could be quite interesting, but also requires an understanding of the origin and formation processes of words. This insight will help to explain the incredible changes in the volume of the English language as well as to predict future trends.

Words are based mostly on Latin and Greek and are formed through several processes. By far, "affixing" is the most common way to build new words. Affixing is the process of placing prefixes or suffixes onto the beginnings or endings of root words. For example, the prefix "micro" placed onto the root word "scope" builds the word "microscope." The suffix "ology" added to "meteor" becomes "meteorology." Examples of affixed words are pretest, preview, hydroplane, biplane, recyclable, biodegradable, chemotherapy, disagreeable, disarm, disarmament, and discomforting. The list contains thousands and thousands more in an expanding list. Obviously, the knowledge of prefix and suffix meanings is a must.

Other word formation processes include the following. "Compounding" is the process of combining two original words to make one new word. Examples are expressway, flagpole, icebreaker, jailbird, manpower, outbreak, and pushcart. Notice the new meanings from the original words. "Borrowed" words mainstreamed directly into English from another language have increased. Examples are shish kebab, pizza, croissant, kamikaze, wok, raccoon, karate, smorgasbord, and snorkel. "Acronyms" are words formed from the first letters of several words. Examples are AIDS (Acquired Immune Deficiency Syndrome), scuba (self contained underwater breathing apparatus), NATO (North Atlantic Treaty Organization), and DARE (Drug and Alcohol Resistance Education). "Initialisms" are words stated as the first letters. Examples are FBI, CIA, EPA. "Blends" merge parts of two words into a new word. Examples are smoke/fog become smog, breakfast/lunch become brunch, capsule/tablet become caplet, camera/recorder become camcorder. Finally, "clipping" is the process of abbreviating words into shorter versions. Examples are bicycle—bike, refrigerator—fridge, professional—pro, temporary or temperature—temp.

There are many reasons for this dynamic expansion of the English language. Technology heads the list with immigration and the American multicultural society a close second. Also, advertising, business, and the world market economy contribute to this expansion. How big will that dictionary be and how long will that final fireworks display last one or two hundred years from now?

## Major/Minor Topics

*1.* List all of the minor topics from the selection for the major topic "Word Formation Processes."

_____

_____

_____

*2.* The major topic for the minor topics "linguist or etymologist" would be (*a*) people who build languages  (*b*) people who study languages  (*c*) people who advertise languages  (*d*) people who write dictionaries.

_____

*3.* Which of the following would be minor topics for the major topic "reasons for the dynamic expansion of the English language"?  (*a*) technology and business  (*b*) multicultural changes and immigration  (*c*) advertising and world markets  (*d*) all of these

_____

## Main Idea and Topic Sentence

4. This selection tells mainly about  (*a*) people  (*b*) ideas  (*c*) changes  (*d*) predictions.

   _____

5. Write a title for this selection.

   _____

6. In which paragraph is the topic sentence NOT the first sentence?  (*a*) 1st (*b*) 2nd  (*c*) 3rd  (*d*) 4th

   _____

   Copy what you think is the topic sentence of that paragraph.

   _____

   _____

## Details

7. How many words were there in the English language in the 1500's?

   _____

8. What three languages are referred to in the selection?

   _____

## Signal Words

9. What two signal words in the second sentence of the first paragraph answer the questions "when" and "how"?

   _____

10. What signal word tells you that "clipping" is the last process given for building new words in the selection?

   _____

### SOCIAL STUDIES PRACTICE A

**PREREADING**  The Bill of Rights and the remaining amendments to the Constitution of the United States guarantee freedoms for every U.S. citizen. Do you know most of these rights?

Bills, bills, bills—how many times do we read about, hear about or experience the consternation of keeping up with those bills? Well, there are some bills that we not only enjoy each day, but are also free! In addition, these bills are the envy of many other countries.

When the Constitution was sent to the states to be signed in 1787, many Americans were not happy. They demanded that a bill, or specific list, of rights be added to the Constitution to protect certain personal rights. Hence, two hundred proposals or amendments were suggested to and discussed by the writers of the Constitution. The final ten agreed upon were presented to the states for signing or ratification in 1791. These ratified amendments became known as the Bill of Rights or the first ten amendments to the what we treasure today as the Constitution of the United States.

Following are those ten rights and a brief summary of each:

Amendment 1. Freedom of Religion, Speech, Press, Assembly, and Petition
This amendment prevents Congress from making any laws to deny such rights.

Amendment 2. Right to Bear Arms
This amendment allows citizens to keep and use guns to protect themselves.

Amendment 3. Housing of Troops
This amendment prevents the government from forcing citizens to keep soldiers in the home without consent of the owner.

Amendment 4. Searches and Seizures
This amendment protects citizens' homes from being searched or private property taken without court permission in the form of a search warrant.

Amendment 5. Rights of Accused Person
This amendment allows a person accused of a crime to have due process of law, except for military related accusations.

Amendment 6. Right to a Speedy, Fair Trial
This amendment allows for a fair trial by jury within the district where the accusation occurred.

Amendment 7. Civil Suits
This amendment allows people with a disagreement of more than $20 to have a trial by jury to reach a decision or judgment.

Amendment 8. Bails, Fines, Punishments
This amendment allows for fair amounts of money for bail or fines or punishments related to due process and return of all bail, if the person shows up for trial.

Amendment 9. Powers Reserved to the People
This amendment allows many other rights for Americans not specifically granted in other amendments. Examples of these rights are the freedom to travel and live anywhere, to work in any job, to marry and raise a family, to receive a public school education, and to join a political party, a union, or other legal group.

Amendment 10. Powers Reserved to the States
This amendment provides states with protection from being sued in courts of other states.

Since 1791, seventeen additional amendments have been added to the Constitution from the Abolition of Slavery in 1865 to Women's Suffrage in 1920. This allowed women to vote for the first time. The most recent was the 27th, on Congressional Pay Raises added in 1992.

No budgeting in the checkbook for these bills—just a lifetime of spending the freedoms ingrained in the Constitution of the United States.

## Major and Minor Topics

1. Which of the following minor topics would NOT be listed under the major topic "rights of the first Amendment to the Constitution"? (*a*) assembly (*b*) religion (*c*) bails (*d*) press

_____

2. The minor topics "Amendments 4, 5, 6 to the Constitution" would fall under the major topic (*a*) Amendments relating to court actions (*b*) Amendments relating to war (*c*) Amendments relating to the states (*d*) Amendments relating to arms.

_____

3. Copy from the selection the examples of Amendments to the Constitution since 1791 and the year for each.

_____

_____

_____

## Main Idea and Topic Sentence

4. This article tells mainly about (*a*) the entire Constitution (*b*) the Bill of Rights (*c*) the ratification of the Constitution (*d*) the right to a fair trial.

_____

5. Using your own words, write a one sentence main idea for this selection.

_____

_____

6. Copy the sentence from the second paragraph that you think is the topic sentence of this paragraph.

_____

_____

_____

## Details

7. When was slavery abolished?  (*a*) 1791  (*b*) 1865  (*c*) 1920  (*d*) 1982

_____

8. How many Amendments to the Constitution are there in total?

_____

## Signal Words

9. What signal word in the second paragraph indicates the results of the states' demand for a list of rights?  (*a*) when  (*b*) or  (*c*) hence  (*d*) and

_____

10. What signal words in the description of Amendment 9 contrast the rights provided?

_____

### SOCIAL STUDIES PRACTICE B

**PREREADING**   American cities and towns are growing old. The time for attending to the different needs is at hand.

The infrastructure of many older American cities and towns is cause for immediate concern and long-range planning. Government officials at all levels, wrestling with solutions, need to take action or prepare citizens for steadily declining services and public properties. Like stretched elastic bands, tax dollars are tightly wound around current budgets.

These constrained budgets allow fewer funds for repairing or replacing deteriorating roads, streets, and sidewalks. Antiquated bridges are also a major transportation and safety concern within this infrastructure. Underground water and sewer lines installed years ago are disintegrating and leaking. Capital improvements to aging public properties such as schools, libraries, and town halls are necessary for the children, parents, and citizens of today and tomorrow. Moreover, parks and playgrounds require attention to be of aesthetic and recreational value to a community.

The dearth of money and planning has affected the environmental qualities of waterways such as rivers, lakes, and ponds. The rapid pollution of these resources unfairly denies future generations of clean water for drinking, swimming, fishing, and boating, not to mention the impact on the beauty of a city or town.

Clearly, time is of the essence. Equally clear is the continuous strain on this infrastructure beyond the yearly budget. Population growth, changing economies with unpredictable taxes, and political squabbling all contribute to this strain on urban America. These problems can be looked upon as pictures of American cities caught in the need to continue to provide a good quality of life and services for their citizens. Hopefully, these pictures will establish priorities for thinking and action by present generations.

## Major and Minor Topics

*1.* List four minor topics from the selection for the major topic "deteriorating infrastructures of older American cities."

_____

_____

*2.* Which of the following major topics would best fit the minor topics "rivers, lakes, ponds" as used in the selection?   (*a*) sources of power   (*b*) sources of travel   (*c*) natural resources for recreation   (*d*) natural resources affected by pollution

_____

*3.* Which of the following is a set of minor topics from the selection for the major topic "contribute to strains on urban America"?   (*a*) pictures, population, politics   (*b*) natural resources, economies, sewer lines   (*c*) population, taxes, politics   (*d*) bridges, libraries, town halls

_____

## Main Idea and Topic Sentence

*4.* This article tells mainly about   (*a*) problems   (*b*) solutions   (*c*) politicians   (*d*) government.

_____

*5.* Write a title of your own for this selection.

_____

_____

*6.* Rewrite the topic sentence in paragraph three into your own words.

_____

_____

_____

## Details

*7.* What specific infrastructures are disintegrating and leaking?

_____

*8.* What word does the author use that means the same as "dearth"?   (*a*) amount   (*b*) gain   (*c*) depth   (*d*) lack

## *Signal Words*

9. What signal word(s) introduce(s) the examples of "public properties" in the selection?

_____

10. What signal word(s) tell(s) you that there are additional "public properties" listed in the selection?

_____

## SOCIAL STUDIES PRACTICE C

**PREREADING** Just because we live in a modern civilization does not mean we know all that there is to know. The unwritten knowledge of other societies is vast and irreplaceable—and it is disappearing.

One horrible day about 1,600 years ago, the wisdom of many centuries went up in flames. The great library in Alexandria burned down, a catastrophe at the time and a symbol for all ages of the vulnerability of human knowledge. The tragedy forced scholars to grope to reconstruct a grand literature and science that once lay neatly catalogued in scrolls.

Today, with little notice, more vast archives of knowledge and expertise are spilling into oblivion, leaving humanity in danger of losing its past and perhaps jeopardizing its future as well. Stored in the memories of elders, healers, midwives, farmers, fishermen, and hunters in the estimated 15,000 cultures remaining on earth is an enormous trove of wisdom.

This largely undocumented knowledge base is humanity's lifeline to a time when people accepted nature's authority and learned through trial, error, and observation. But the world's tribes are dying out or being absorbed into modern civilization. As they vanish, so does their irreplaceable knowledge.

Over the ages, indigenous peoples have developed innumerable technologies and arts. They have devised ways to farm deserts without irrigation and produce abundance from the rain forest without destroying the delicate balance that maintains the ecosystem; they have learned how to navigate vast distances in the Pacific using their knowledge of currents and the feel of intermittent waves that bounce off distant islands; they have explored the medicinal properties of plants; and they have acquired an understanding of the basic ecology of flora and fauna. If this knowledge had to be duplicated from scratch, it would put the scientific resources of the West to shame. Much of this expertise and wisdom has already disappeared, and if neglected, most of the remainder could be gone within the next generation.

## Major/Minor Topics

1. Write a major topic of your own using information from the selection for the minor topics "elders, healers, midwives, farmers, fishermen, and hunters."

_____

2. Which of the following would be a major topic for the minor topics "trial, error, and observation"? (*a*) information lost in the catastrophe at Alexandria (*b*) irreplaceable knowledge of the 15,000 cultures (*c*) how people learned in the 15,000 cultures (*d*) innumerable technologies and arts of the 15,000 cultures

_____

3. List three minor topics from the selection for the major topic "technologies, arts, expertise, and wisdom of indigenous peoples."

_____

_____

_____

## Main Idea and Topic Sentence

4. Which of the following titles do you think best fits this selection? (*a*) Lost Cultures Means Lost Knowledge (*b*) Library Tragedy Destroys Literature and Science Information (*c*) Humanity Doomed as Civilizations Disappear (*d*) Arts and Technologies Outdated in Most Cultures

_____

5. Which paragraph do you think contains the LEAST amount of information related to the main idea of the selection? (*a*) 1st (*b*) 2nd (*c*) 3rd (*d*) 4th

_____

6. Copy a topic sentence from the selection that you think could also be the main idea of the selection.

_____

_____

_____

## Details

7. Where was literature and science once specifically catalogued? (*a*) in Alexandria (*b*) on islands (*c*) in flora (*d*) in scrolls

_____

8. What do indigenous peoples maintain in the rain forest? (*a*) irrigation (*b*) ecosystem (*c*) navigation (*d*) medicinal properties

_____

## *Signal Words*

**9.** What signal word is used in the second paragraph to keep the focus on the present tense?   (*a*) today   (*b*) more   (*c*) as well   (*d*) and

_____

**10.** What two signal words are used in the concluding sentence to explain "amount"?

_____


## SCIENCE PRACTICE A

**PREREADING**   Do you have a computer at school or at home? Whether you do or not, you also have a computer that goes with you wherever you go. It is inside your head.

Think about the most complicated computer on earth. Now consider that the power to generate that very thought begins in that very same computer! Yes, the human brain truly is a wondrously constructed marvel of nature. To understand the mind is to understand its main parts and workings. This complicated control center of the body and its clocklike operation of functions is made up of three parts.

The upper portion of the brain is the *cerebrum*. It controls muscle movement and speech. Also, the cerebrum responds to and interprets messages from the sense organs telling what is hot, cold, delicious, painful, and so on. Most important, the cerebrum oversees intelligence and thus, allows thinking, reasoning, and remembering. The cerebrum is divided into two sections. The left half controls the right side of the body, while the right half controls the left side of the body.

The *cerebellum* is located below the cerebrum and at the back of the head. Much smaller than the cerebrum, the cerebellum controls and adjusts nerve impulses that begin in the cerebrum. These impulses travel rapidly in networks throughout the body, keeping motor coordination or balance smooth and graceful. Otherwise, movement of the limbs and body would be extremely erratic.

The cerebrum and cerebellum are encased in the skull and connected to the spinal cord by the third major part, the *medulla*. The medulla automatically controls the involuntary performance of the body to digest food, sustain breathing, maintain blood pressure, and keep normal heart rate.

Can one imagine for a moment the second-to-second uninterrupted service that this marvelous creation performs? Think about the brain's level of performance with little help or support needed from the outside world. Think about it!

## Major and Minor Topics

1. The major topic for the minor topics "controls movement, oversees intelligence, allows reasoning" would be   (*a*) functions of the spinal cord   (*b*) functions of the medulla   (*c*) functions of the cerebellum   (*d*) functions of the cerebrum.

2. Specific minor topics for the major topic "what the medulla controls" would be   (*a*) remembering, motor coordination, blood pressure   (*b*) digests food, sustains breathing, keeps normal heart rate   (*c*) adjusts nerve impulses, controls sense organs, allows thinking   (*d*) controls speech, digests food, sustains breathing.

3. Write your own major topic for the minor topics "cerebrum, cerebellum, medulla."

## Main Idea and Topic Sentence

4. The main idea of the selection is best stated as   (*a*) how to repair problems in the brain   (*b*) how to make computers like the brain   (*c*) how the brain functions   (*d*) how to protect the brain.

5. Which two sentences in the first paragraph could serve as the topic sentence of the whole selection?   (*a*) 1, 3   (*b*) 2, 3   (*c*) 2, 4   (*d*) 4, 5

6. Which sentence in paragraphs 2, 3, and 4 is the topic sentence?   (*a*) first   (*b*) last   (*c*) a combination of first and last   (*d*) a combination of any sentences

## Details

7. How many parts or sections are there in the cerebrum?   (*a*) 1   (*b*) 2   (*c*) 3   (*d*) too many to count

8. What does the medulla connect the brain to?   (*a*) the skull   (*b*) the cerebrum   (*c*) the network of nerves   (*d*) the spinal cord

## Signal Words

**9.** What signal words does the author use to explain that "intelligence" is the major function of the cerebrum?

_____

**10.** What signal word does the author use to explain "how" the medulla controls its functions? (***a***) rapidly (***b***) automatically (***c***) importantly (***d***) thus

_____

### SCIENCE PRACTICE B

**PREREADING**   Physical science is the study of the earth and its parts. Understanding these parts allows you to learn about the complexities and balance of the earth's chemistry.

The earth is made of many different parts and the name of all its parts together is *matter*. Matter can be defined as anything that has weight and takes up space; thus land, water, and air are all examples of matter. They have differences that we can see, because one is a solid, one is a liquid, and one is a gas. These forms—solid, liquid, gas—are the three states of matter.

Although different kinds of matter look different, they all have something in common. All matter is made of elements, which are combinations of small particles called *atoms*. An atom is the smallest unit of matter.

Since there are only ninety-two natural elements, how can the earth contain so many different kinds of matter? This variety is possible because elements combine to make different substances. Matter that is formed from two or more elements is called a *compound*. Compounds may be very different from the elements that go into them, just as a cake is very different from the eggs, flour, and milk that go into it. Salt, for example, is a compound that is formed from sodium and chlorine. Each of these is a poisonous element, but when the two are combined, they are used as a seasoning for food.

The smallest unit of a compound is called a *molecule*. If a molecule is taken apart, it will no longer be a compound. It will be a group of separate elements. Scientists use abbreviations to name compounds to tell what elements are in each compound. They also tell how many atoms of each element are present in one molecule of the compound. For example, the compound of sodium chloride is written NaCl.

The earth has a complex, but balanced, chemistry of its own. Understanding some components of this chemistry such as matter, elements, compounds, and molecules will help in understanding the physical science of this delicately balanced planet.

## *Major and Minor Topics*

1. What is the major topic for the minor topics "land, water, air"?

   _____

2. The minor topics for the major topic "states of matter" are  (*a*) eggs, flour, milk  (*b*) space, weight, land  (*c*) solid, liquid, gas  (*d*) elements, molecules, atoms.

   _____

## *Main Idea and Topic Sentence*

3. Copy the one sentence from the entire selection that would best serve as a main idea sentence.

   _____

4. The topic sentence in each paragraph in this selection is usually  (*a*) the first sentence  (*b*) the last sentence  (*c*) a middle sentence  (*d*) a combination of all of the above.

   _____

## *Details*

5. How many elements are needed to make a compound? _____

6. When separate, sodium and chlorine are  (*a*) poisonous  (*b*) elements  (*c*) the abbreviations Na and Cl  (*d*) all of these.

   _____

7. What is the smallest unit of a compound called?

   _____

8. How many natural elements are there on earth? _____

## *Signal Words*

9. What signal word used in the selection tells you that salt is a compound formed from sodium and chlorine?  (*a*) for example  (*b*) or  (*c*) but  (*d*) also

   _____

10. What two conjunction signal words are used in the last paragraph and what function do these words perform in order of use?

    _____

    _____

## SCIENCE PRACTICE C

**PREREADING**  Lead poisoning is a major health threat to all Americans, especially young children. Learn about this threat and how to avoid it.

Next time you see a person in a white lab coat scrutinizing an area and spooning soil samples into sealed containers, the catalyst for such action might be more obvious. A distressing current health hazard is a poison embedded in the topsoil along freeways and highways. It has settled into the grounds of traffic-congested inner cities. It is also the bane of older dwellings with interior paint applied before the 1950's. What is this silent and potentially damaging dread? It is lead, and it is not biodegradable.

Lead was a common additive in many commonly used products during much of the 20th century. Gasoline for added performance and paint for durability were the most common "leaded" products. Regulations prohibiting leaded products were mandated in the 1950's for paints and in the 1980's for gasolines. Scientists and doctors are especially worried about the effect of lead on children up to six years old who play in dirt contaminated by years of auto emissions filled with microscopic particles of lead. The other alarming situation is the number of youngsters who eat the sweet-tasting chips of paint, saturated with lead, from woodwork or ceilings.

Levels of lead in soil and products or in blood tests for children are measured in "parts per million" or "ppm." Safe and normal levels measure about 20 ppm, but many samples and patients today show levels from 100 to 6600 ppm! Readings over 500 ppm are considered a major threat. Children who ingest such volumes of contamination face likely brain disorders, nervous system disfunction, or learning disabilities during school years. These maladies are irreversible!

There are new laws for deleading homes and businesses in contrast to the lack of attention paid to lead in the ground of neighborhoods. The EPA (Environmental Protection Agency) does have "superfunds" for critical cleanup of known hazardous waste sites. However, little attention is paid to neighborhood lead cleanups. Perhaps superfund monies could be extended for such use in the future. Regardless of government action or inaction, thousands of young children face health problems, and just as many adults painfully experience the effects of lead poisoning for a lifetime. Monitoring of children's activities and testing are important, but prevention through cleanup is more important.

## *Major and Minor Topics*

1.  What is the major topic for the minor topics "freeways, highways, cities, dwellings" as used in this selection?  (*a*) areas of growth in the 20th century  (*b*) areas of lead cleanup in the 20th century  (*c*) areas of lead contamination in the 20th century  (*d*) none of these

2. Give the two minor topics from the selection for the major topic "dates and products requiring deleading."

_____

_____

3. Give each of the health threats to children who ingest high levels of lead.

_____

_____

_____

## Main Idea and Topic Sentence

4. Which of the following phrases would least relate to the main idea of the selection? (*a*) soil samples  (*b*) interior of dwellings  (*c*) auto emissions  (*d*) woodwork or ceilings

_____

5. Write a title of your own for this selection.

_____

6. Choose a topic sentence from the selection and rewrite it into your own words.

_____

_____

_____

## Details

7. What kind of test is referred to in the selection?

_____

8. What are "maladies"?  (*a*) disorders  (*b*) tests  (*c*) sites  (*d*) funds

_____

## Signal Words

9. Underline the adverb and conjunction signal words in the following sentence. Then write each word and its function. "Safe and normal levels measure about 20 ppm, but many samples and patients today show levels from 100 to 6600 ppm."

_____

10. What does the signal word "however" contrast as used in the last paragraph?

_____

_____

# Thinking and Learning Activities
*Complete independently or in cooperative groups*

## WITHIN A SELECTION (SEE SCIENCE PRACTICE A)

**1. Know** Define two functions for each part of the brain under the major topic "Functions of the Brain's Three Parts."

**2. Comprehend** Identify and copy one sentence that you think could serve as the title of the selection. Write it in capital letters.

**3. Apply** Exhibit one picture of the brain from a book or a drawing of your own and write one main idea sentence related to what you see and know.

**4. Analyze** Arrange the functions for each part of the brain in order of importance using numbers and function under each part.

**5. Synthesize** Compose a poem of four to eight lines about the brain, using information in the selection. Give your poem a title.

**6. Evaluate** Decide in which section of the brain you would accept reduced performance. Give three minor topic reasons for your answer. Put the reasons in complete sentences with the most important first.

## BEYOND A SELECTION (SEE SOCIAL STUDIES A)

**1. Know** Label Amendments 11–27 by number and name and ratification date. Use a history book or appropriate reference material.

**2. Comprehend** Summarize in one paragraph a media story about the Constitution or an amendment or a violation of rights. Use a good topic sentence, several detailed supporting sentences, and a good concluding sentence.

**3. Apply** Interview a lawyer or court official to find one example of how each first amendment right could be denied. Write one detailed sentence for each of the five rights.

**4. Analyze** Organize the rights of Amendment 9 in order of importance in your life as you see it now. Use the major topic "The 9th Amendment in My Life."

**5. Synthesize** Create a situation at home or at school or at work that violates your rights under one amendment. In a detailed paragraph explain the situation, the violation, and the amendment involved. Follow proper paragraph structure of topic, supporting, and concluding sentences.

**6. Evaluate** Predict the 28th Amendment to the Constitution. Give details, dates, topics, and descriptions in a paragraph with the main idea or title "The 28th Amendment to the Constitution."

## ABOUT A SELECTION (SEE LANGUAGE ARTS C)

Use a variety of sources such as dictionaries, textbooks, newspapers, magazines, television, or even selections in this book as reference materials. Read and gather examples of words showing the word formation processes for the following project.

**Part 1**   List several examples for each major topic of the word formation processes. For example: "Examples of Affixed Words," "Examples of Compound Words," "Examples of Borrowed Words."

**Part 2**   List 5–10 additional new examples for a particular word formation process in one area or subject. For example: "Affixed Business Words," "Government Acronyms," "Sports Compound Words."

**Part 3**   Design a unique new product or invention and write a detailed paragraph describing it and its functions. Use words that exist and/or make up original new words, from a variety of word formation processes, in your description of the product or invention.

Consider defining words that may require some explanation in each part above.

# Unit lll
# ORGANIZATIONAL PATTERN SKILLS

## Overview the Skills

### 1. SEQUENCE

Sequence is simply the order of events occurring in a written selection. Sometimes, the author will present this order in specific time structure called "chronological" order, such as the time of day or the days of the week or a list of years.

Understanding sequence in written material is easy when you think about how the skill works in daily routines. For example, think about the sequence of events for washing a car or preparing for a test or following the class schedule in a day at school.

Put the following account of events that caused the Civil War into correct sequence by rearranging the order of numbers:

1. The great debate between Lincoln and Douglas took place in 1858.
2. The book *Uncle Tom's Cabin* was written in 1852 and showed accounts of slavery that infuriated the North.
3. John Brown attempts to free slaves at Harper's Ferry in 1859.
4. The Kansas-Nebraska Act of 1854 allowed these states to have the option of choosing slavery.
5. Abraham Lincoln was elected President in 1860.

Notice how chronological order enabled you to choose the correct sequence.

### On Your Own

Complete the following list with events of your own. You may include chronological references.

1. Commencement weekend was about to begin with graduation ceremonies scheduled for Friday evening at 7:30 p.m.
2. Saturday morning would include senior breakfast at 10:00 a.m. and the oceanside class trip with beach activities beginning at noon.

3. _____

_____

4. _____

_____

5. _____

_____

## 2. THE 5 W's AND LISTING

The author often uses two simple but effective tools to present information to you. The use of the "5 W's pattern" and "Listing" organizes this information and allows you to better understand what you read and to better organize what you write.

The 5 W's are WHO, WHAT, WHERE, WHEN, and WHY. In order, these W's indicate the person or people, the action, the place, the time, and the reason. For example, notice the 5 W's in such order in the following sentence:

(WHO) Meteorologists (WHAT) study weather patterns (WHERE) around the country (WHEN) every hour (WHY) because pilots need constant updates for airline safety.

The 5 W's can be put in any order. Find the order of the 5 W's when the sentence is rewritten as follows:

Because pilots need constant updates for airline safety, meteorologists every hour study weather patterns around the country.

Let's add a listing to our model sentence, allowing the sentence to contain more information in the WHY section.

Meteorologists study weather patterns around the country every hour because pilots, navigators, controllers, and ground personnel need constant updates for airline safety.

Remember that a sentence about people need only contain two of the 5 W's— WHO and WHAT—to function as a complete sentence.

### On Your Own

1. Add the other 3 W's and a listing of your own to the following sentence:

Researchers study diseases.

_____

_____

2. Now rewrite the sentence by rearranging the 5 W's.

_____

_____

## 3. COMPARISON AND CONTRAST; CAUSE AND EFFECT

Authors use "comparison and contrast" patterns to indicate what is alike and different. We constantly use this skill during all tasks to find likenesses and differences in characteristics of food, clothing, people, household items, appliances, and so on. The following sentence is an example of the pattern: The World Series and the Superbowl are America's two most favorite sporting events, but the World Series is probably number one because of its longer history and the status of baseball.

The "cause and effect" pattern organizes events into series of reasons (causes) and results (effects). We know that Pearl Harbor was bombed in 1941 and the result was the United States' declaration of war against Japan.

Again, these patterns of organization allow you to better understand what you read and more effectively organize what you write.

A. Notice the following examples of comparison and contrast.

Biologists study animals and plants. Psychologists study human behavior and the mind.

World Wars I and II were supported by the American people, while the Vietnam War was not.

B. Now notice examples of cause and effect

The severe summer drought caused higher food prices during the fall and winter months.

The opportunities for a better life have brought immigrants to the United States since colonial days.

### On Your Own

1. Write a sentence or two of your own with comparisons and contrasts for the topics "cable TV vs. regular channels" or "VCR vs. movie theaters."

_____

_____

_____

2. Now use the same topics to write a sentence or two with causes and effects.

_____

_____

_____

# Practice the Skills

**PREREADING**   Remember those Halloween nights as a child and the images of witches and witchcraft? What is the actual past, present, and future story of this occult craft?

The execution of Joan of Arc in 1431, Shakespeare's Macbeth in 1606, and Salem, Massachusetts, in the late 1600's all spin the history of witchcraft into a fabric of interesting practices and study. Witches were scorned people, usually women. They were empowered with supernatural forces allowing them to cast spells and curses that caused loss of property and personal suffering for victims. People believed these allies of Satan could invoke powers. These powers could allow witches to change the weather, become invisible, fly on brooms, and turn enemies into animals.

The public hysteria over witchcraft reached its height in Europe and America in the 1600's and 1700's. Many, many thousands of convicted witches were tortured and put to death throughout Europe during this period. Most were hanged or burned at the stake. These suspected sorceresses were most often found guilty with little or nothing more than gossip and coincidence as evidence.

Colonists brought the belief to America in the 1600's. People with devil marks such as scars, moles, or birthmarks were immediate suspects of practicing the satanic art. Cotton Mather was a fire-and-brimstone preacher during this Puritan time in American history. He was a driving force in the late 1600's in Salem, Massachusetts. Mather's Sunday sermons used the widespread public phobia of witches to incite action against them. In 1692 a witch-hunt resulted in 19 executions after a mockery of the trial process, while 150 others were imprisoned for many years. These trials have become a blemish on American history, but have also created a source of historical curiosity and daily tourism for Salem, Massachusetts.

Witches and the craft still exist in America and around the world today. It is recognized as an organized religion complete with meetings and festivals called Witches' Sabbaths. Education, television, movies, and books have reduced the ignorance and fear of this occult practice. The stereotype of the modern witch is one of a different sort of individual who causes little harm and even less fear in the minds of others. It is Halloween, coupled with the actual practice of modern witchcraft, that can serve as vivid reminders of hocus-pocus, magic potions, demons and black cats, and the age-old presence of witchcraft—either real or conjured in the minds of superstitious observers.

## Sequence

1. Using information from the selection, when did Cotton Mather influence the history of witchcraft? (*a*) before the execution of Joan of Arc (*b*) after the Salem witch trials (*c*) after Shakespeare's Macbeth (*d*) before Shakespeare's Macbeth

2. When was witchcraft brought to America? (*a*) before it reached its peak in Europe (*b*) about the same time it was at its peak in Europe (*c*) after it peaked in Europe (*d*) after 1692

3. The events in sequence of a Salem witch hunt according to the selection included which one of the following? (*a*) sermon, action, execution, trial (*b*) action, trial, sermon, execution (*c*) sermon, action, trial, execution (*d*) none of these

## 5 W's and Listing

4. Which one of the 5 W's is missing from the following sentence? "Many, many thousands of convicted witches were tortured and put to death throughout Europe during this period." (*a*) Why (*b*) When (*c*) Where (*d*) What (*e*) Who

5. How many of the 5 W's are included in the following sentence? "He was a driving force in the late 1600's in Salem, Massachusetts." (*a*) 2 (*b*) 3 (*c*) 4 (*d*) 5

6. List all of the things from the selection that have reduced the ignorance and fear of witchcraft today.

## Comparison and Contrast; Cause and Effect

7. The best comparison of witchcraft in Europe and America during the 1600's, according to information in the selection, probably involved (*a*) the types of curses (*b*) the trial process (*c*) the speeches of Cotton Mather (*d*) the number of executions.

8. The best contrast between witchcraft in the 1600's and today would be which of the following? (*a*) ignorance of witchcraft is reduced today (*b*) witchcraft was more organized in the 1600's (*c*) actual witches are not as appealing today (*d*) Sabbaths were more common in the 1600's

9. What was the cause of Cotton Mather's success as a preacher? (*a*) 19 executions (*b*) television and movies (*c*) historical curiosity (*d*) public phobia of witches

10. What effect do the Salem witch trials of 1692 have on Salem, Massachusetts, today according to the selection? (*a*) no effect (*b*) increased history books (*c*) increased tourism (*d*) annual witch festivals

# Applying the Skills in Content Subjects

## LANGUAGE ARTS PRACTICE A

**PREREADING** Think about a favorite fairy tale you remember from childhood days. Sometimes real life experiences become a fairy tale come true.

Who said that fairy tales are only make-believe? Ms. Jill Weiner fulfilled a lifelong dream and became an elementary teacher in the northeastern United States for several years. However, the loss of her job due to budget reductions and the acceptance by graduate school in Kentucky brought changes in routine, planning, life-style, and surroundings. Two years later, with advanced degree in hand and few teaching positions at home, Jill applied abroad. A local school district on the outskirts of London, England, welcomed her background and experience with open arms and extended the opportunity once again to teach younger children. Into a brand new life she eagerly settled with youthful enthusiasm toward a new country and vocation. Jill also maintained her love for academic endeavor and thus enrolled in part-time study at a nearby university for two evenings per week to enrich skills, meet new friends, and become familiar with English customs.

Flight Lieutenant Andrew Hill was a career pilot for the RAF (Royal Air Force). He lived 50 miles north of London and made the daily commute by train to the airbase outside London. There, Lt. Hill flew his GR-5 Harrier jet in short maneuvers and missions called sorties. He flew these sorties to keep his skills honed and the squadron prepared for any military urgency. Conflicting work and commuting schedules caused later jaunts home two nights each week. To both occupy this time and add credits toward a degree, Andrew Hill enrolled in courses at the same university as Jill.

Lt. Andrew Hill and Ms. Jill Weiner met at the university, dated for one year, and were engaged to marry. The ceremony was performed in the States and was distinguished with all the taste and splendor of American and British custom. The bride graced the setting with the traditional white gown that complemented the beauty and charm of her personality. The groom was resplendently dressed in full military uniform. His confident manner was complete with the four-foot, gold-handled, stainless steel ceremonial sword that characterized his rank. The guests were assembled in a modern-day Shangri-la.

## Sequence

1. Which of the following are in proper sequence regarding Jill's experiences? (*a*) graduate school, marriage, London teaching job   (*b*) lost job at home, met Andrew Hill, attended London university   (*c*) advanced degree, London teaching job, met Andrew Hill   (*d*) marriage, returned home, attended London university

_____

2. The sequence of events for Lt. Hill twice weekly included which of the following? (*a*) commute, fly, school, commute   (*b*) school, commute, fly, commute (*c*) commute, school, fly, commute   (*d*) none of these

_____

3. What were the three events in correct sequence from the selection relating to Jill and Andrew's relationship before marriage?

_____

_____

_____

## 5 W's and Listing

4. Rewrite the second sentence of the selection into a new order of WHEN, WHERE, WHO, WHAT.

_____

_____

5. Which three of the 5 W's are in the following sentence? "The guests were assembled in a modern-day Shangri-la."   (*a*) Who, what, why   (*b*) Who, when, where (*c*) Who, what, where   (*d*) Who, what, when

_____

6. List the reasons from the selection for Jill's attending the university in England.

_____

_____

## Comparison and Contrast; Cause and Effect

7. Would you compare or contrast Jill's two jobs as explained in the selection?

_____

Explain your answer.

_____

_____

**8.** Contrast Andrew Hill's two methods of transportation during the average working day.

_____

_____

**9.** What was the cause of Jill's loss of job at home? (*a*) acceptance by graduate school (*b*) changes in life-style (*c*) budget reductions (*d*) all of these

_____

**10.** Explain two effects from the selection related to Lt. Hill's missions or sorties.

_____

_____

## LANGUAGE ARTS PRACTICE B

**PREREADING** Bicycling is the most common form of transportation in the world. Once a year, it also becomes a major international sporting event.

The roads go up, and the roads go down. They twist and they turn, past fields of sunflowers in the middle of nowhere and past throngs of spectators in the center of Dijon. It's sweater weather on the top of a mountain, and it's hot enough to melt asphalt in the valley below.

The race does not discriminate. The race filters out any mediocre riders so that only the elite are left by the time the competitors get to Paris. The race is the Tour de France.

Today, bicyclists will start the journey and they will take a spin around Lyons, southeast of Paris. This race is called a "prologue," really just for show, a preliminary time trial to kick off the Tour. Tomorrow, the almost 200 riders get serious. They'll have one race in the morning, another in the afternoon, and are on their way for a grueling tour of France. The course will be sometimes rugged and sometimes scenic, but one thing is certain—it will always be a blur for the riders.

The Tour changes slightly every year, although some things are constant. Taking a cue from its name, the Tour de France takes three weeks to span the country. One year it goes clockwise; the next counterclockwise. This year the racers will start south of Paris, in Lyons, then travel north to the Normandy area, west toward Brittany, then fly south to Pau, where they begin their hardest tests in the Pyrenees and Alps before taking a train overnight and then riding their last day to the welcoming spectators in Paris. About two-thirds of the 198 who begin the race will finish the 3,940-kilometer race; others will drop out because of injury, exhaustion, or simply not qualifying, which means finishing the day's race within a certain percentage of the winner.

## Sequence

1. The sequence of time in the third paragraph is  (*a*) yesterday, today, tomorrow  (*b*) today, tomorrow, next year  (*c*) today, tomorrow morning, tomorrow afternoon  (*d*) tomorrow morning, tomorrow afternoon, tomorrow evening.

2. List three events in sequence from the selection related to this year's race once it begins.

3. What event in the selection takes place just before the riders are welcomed in Paris?  (*a*) a train ride  (*b*) a test in the Alps  (*c*) a prologue  (*d*) a time trial

## 5 W's and Listing

4. Add the necessary information of your own so that the following sentence then has all 5 W's and makes sense. "Tomorrow, the almost 200 riders get serious."

5. Copy five phrases from the selection that tell WHERE.

6. List the three reasons from the selection that cause riders to drop out of the race.

## Comparison and Contrast; Cause and Effect

7. The first paragraph contains several comparisons and contrasts relating mostly to  (*a*) people  (*b*) distances  (*c*) geography  (*d*) clothing.

8. The most consistent contrast in the race from year to year is about  (*a*) direction  (*b*) number of contestants  (*c*) scenery  (*d*) distance of race.

9. What is the effect of a rider not finishing the day's race within a certain percentage of the winner?

_____

10. Why is the "prologue" appropriately named?

_____

_____

_____

## LANGUAGE ARTS PRACTICE C

**PREREADING**   How often do you wish for money or power? To what extent would you go to have such a wish come true?

H. Harrison Houston knew that these were not encouraging times at school, work, and home. As he inched through the turnstile and into a sea of humanity, the subway doors yawned open. Harrison angled arms and legs through the tightly knit crowd and settled quickly into the remaining seat with peculiar amazement that such a vacancy existed. He observed the rainbow of riders each day on the transit route and the consistent display from poverty to wealth. Harrison understood the poverty and envied the wealth.

Sensing that his observations, thoughts, and feelings were transmitting to some other rider, Harrison cautiously glanced right. There sat a very old man, threadbare in dress, and heavy in breathing. The eye contact lasted several seconds, but an eternity of communication occupied the moment. From a tattered and torn pocket, a scarlet-red card with bold black lettering found its way into Harrison's notebook. At the next stop, company parted as Harrison bounded off the train, up the stairs, and into the sunshine with curiosity flooding his mind.

An abandoned storefront provided solitude for Harrison to reduce the floodgates in one reading. I KNOW YOU, BUT YOU DON'T KNOW ME . . . THAT MYSTERY FOREVER SHALL BE. Harrison, somewhat befuddled, turned the card over. REPEAT THESE WORDS IN FRONT OF A MIRROR WHILE ALONE, AND FORTUNE WILL BE YOURS, BUT NOT WITHOUT THE LOSS OF SOMEONE YOU KNOW! He would repeat these words in front of a mirror to gain fortune? How simple, Harrison mused.

At 7:30 that Friday eve, Harrison anxiously peered at his image and furtively repeated the black inscription. At 9:40, a radio station informed Harrison that a family Caribbean vacation was the result of a randomly chosen phone number. At 10:10, a telegram arrived telling of the passing of an aunt not seen in years by Harrison. He was awestruck! Despite a tossing and turning night, Saturday's events included the recitation, a winning lottery ticket, and the accidental death of a neighbor for whom

Harrison had little regard. Harrison performed the Sunday morning reading and was awarded a bonus at work. His grandfather died at the hospital that night from heart failure. Harrison's grandfather thought much of his first grandchild. Monday included the verbal exercise, a scholarship at school, and a transit authority afternoon call to the Houston family.

The Tuesday morning headlines sensationalized the event of a young man who either fell or was pushed from the platform into the path of an oncoming train during the rush hour. The bold black lettering stood in stark contrast to the white background of page 27—Houston, H. Harrison.

## Sequence

1. Rewrite the following events from the first paragraph in the proper sequence: settled into a seat, inched through turnstile, observed the riders, moved into a sea of humanity, angled through the crowd

   *angled through the crowd, inched through the turnstile, moved into a sea of humanity, settled in the seat* see the crowd

2. Refer to the selection for the appropriate events to fill the chronological order of the following:

   Friday at 7:30

   *Harrison peered at his image*

   Friday at 9:40

   *radio informed harrison*

   Friday at 10:10

   *got telegram*

3. Refer to the selection for two events, one good and one bad, to fill the chronological order of the following:

   Saturday

   *winning lotery ticket*
   *didn't win*

   Sunday

   *reward bounus*
   *granddad died*

   Monday

   *scholarship for school*
   *pay a lot*

## 5 W's and Listing

4. How many of the 5 W's are missing in the following sentence? "He would repeat these words in front of the mirror to gain fortune?"

*3*

Rewrite the sentence with appropriate information to complete the 5-W pattern.

*James would repeat these words at 10 am in front of the mirror.*

5. What is the order of the 5 W's in the following sentence? "His grandfather died at the hospital that night from heart failure."

*Who, where, when, why, what*

Rewrite the sentence by rearranging the order of the 5 W's.

*His grandfather had heart failure at night in the hospital*

6. List the three things that Harrison sensed were transmitted to the old man on the subway train.

*observations, thoughts and feelings*

## Comparison and Contrast; Cause and Effect

7. What event is most consistent from day to day after Harrison receives the card? (*a*) the type of fortune  (*b*) the relationship to victims  (*c*) reading the card  (*d*) discussions with family

8. Write one sentence contrasting the scene in the subway in the first and last paragraphs.

*in the oncoming train at rush hour...*

9. What caused the old man to place the card in Harrison's notebook?

*He's related*

10. What ultimate effect did the card have on Harrison?  (*a*) it killed him  (*b*) it brought wealth for the Houston family  (*c*) it made the headlines  (*d*) it was referred to on page 27

## SOCIAL STUDIES PRACTICE A

**PREREADING**   American history is filled with heroic accounts of exploration and triumph. A young native American Indian woman made such a contribution some two centuries ago.

The adventures of Meriwether Lewis and William Clark in exploring the northwestern United States are legendary. Many people do not realize, however, that their journey might have been cut short, a failure, if it hadn't been for the help of an Indian woman who acted as their interpreter and guide. That woman was Sacagawea. Sacagawea was born into the Shoshone tribe, probably about 1787 or 1789. As a young girl, she was captured by an enemy tribe and sold into slavery. She later married a trader named Toussaint Charbonneau.

Before beginning their expedition, Lewis and Clark spent the winter at the fort where Sacagawea lived with her husband. They hired Sacagawea and Charbonneau as interpreters for the expedition because they spoke several Indian languages. When they left, Sacagawea strapped her small baby on her back and carried him for many months during the trek.

The diaries of Lewis and Clark tell much about Sacagawea's help in the expedition. Her background was particularly valuable when the party neared the territory of the Shoshone Indians, Sacagawea's own tribe. The explorers badly needed horses and guides to help them across the Rocky Mountains. As they came upon a Shoshone camp, Sacagawea gave a cry of joy. "We are of one family," she cried—the chief was her brother, whom she had not seen in many years. The tribal council agreed to supply the horses and the guides the explorers needed.

Sacagawea's exploits have been the inspiration for many legends and folk tales. No one knows exactly how much is fact and how much is fiction. But the courage of this young woman in exploring the West is well-remembered. More statues and memorials have been erected to honor Sacagawea than any other American woman.

## *Sequence*

1. As a young girl, the sequence of events in the selection related to Sacagawea's life were   (*a*) married Charbonneau, sold into slavery, captured by tribe   (*b*) captured by tribe, married Charbonneau, sold into slavery   (*c*) captured by tribe, sold into slavery, married Charbonneau   (*d*) none of these.

2. Before the expedition began, which of the following events occurred in sequence for Lewis and Clark?   (*a*) stayed at the fort, looked for horses   (*b*) hired Sacagawea, wrote diary   (*c*) crossed the Rocky Mountains, met the chief   (*d*) stayed at the fort, hired Sacagawea

3. What is the last event from the selection having to do with Lewis and Clark?

## 5 W's and Listing

4. What is the order of the W's in the following sentence? "Sacagawea was born into the Shoshone tribe, probably about 1787 or 1789."

_____

5. Which W's are not included in the following sentence? "She later married a trader named Toussaint Charbonneau."

_____

6. List the two things in the selection needed to cross the Rocky Mountains.

_____

## Comparison and Contrast; Cause and Effect

7. The best comparison of Sacagawea to Lewis and Clark would relate to
(*a*) keeping diaries   (*b*) understanding Indian languages   (*c*) willingness to explore   (*d*) all of these.

_____

8. The main contrast between Lewis and Clark from the beginning and end of the selection relates to their   (*a*) exploring accomplishments   (*b*) communication accomplishments   (*c*) statues and memorials erected   (*d*) folk-tale accomplishments.

_____

9. What was the cause of Sacagawea's "cry of joy" in the selection?

_____

_____

10. List two effects from the selection that result from Sacagawea's exploits today.

_____

_____

## SOCIAL STUDIES PRACTICE B

**PREREADING**   Let's have a geography and history lesson about the "land down under." It's a land of crocodiles and kangaroos and the only island continent we know as Australia.

Early geographers and cartographers believed that there had to be another continent south of the equator to keep the earth balanced. Known as "the land down under" and symbolized by the crocodile and kangaroo, Australia was the last continent settled, except of course for Antarctica. The European explorers of the 1700's found most of Australia to be worthless land and much of this island continent remains barren today. However, present day Australia is also a mirror of contrast to those early observations.

Geographically, Australia compares to the United States in size, but contrasts in terrain. Most of Australia is flat with only one significant mountain range—the Great Dividing Range. Australians appreciate these peaks because they block the westerly sea winds and keep the rainfall in the east for the benefit of agriculture and tourism. Few live in the interior or "outback" because of the arid conditions. Skirting this area are farms and grazing for sheep and cattle. It is the eastern coast that boasts the agricultural and economic lifeline of the country. Here lie the major cities of Sydney, Melbourne, Perth, and the capital, Canberra.

Historically, settlement and population grew as a result of three events. First, England emptied its jails in the late 1700's and shipped these outcasts to Australia. In the early 1800's, many English sought a new life in Australia because of a new breed of sheep called merinos. They were valued for their wool and, later, mutton. In 1851 a prospector unearthed gold west of Sydney, and the influx of miners from England, Scotland, Ireland, and China doubled the population to 1 million. By the late 1800's, most Australians were natives and sought independence. England obliged and the six colonies were united under one constitution in 1901.

Today, Australia is a country of magnificent coastlines, bustling seaports, sprawling cities with forests of skyscrapers, and a total array of business and agricultural opportunity. It is also a tourist mecca for visitors from around the world who arrive daily to discover the flavor of the "land down under," catch a glimpse of a kangaroo or croc, and enjoy the balance of life on the only island continent.

## Sequence

1. Which of the following sets of topics related to Australia's history is in correct sequence? (*a*) gold rush, independence, merinos (*b*) outcasts, independence, merinos (*c*) merinos, gold rush, independence (*d*) independence, merinos, gold rush

2. What two events occurred in sequence during 1851 in Australia?

3. The first event listed in the 1900's in the selection related to Australia's (*a*) business growth (*b*) independence (*c*) tourism development (*d*) population growth

## 5 W's and Listing

4. Which one of the 5 W's is missing in the following sentence? "Few live in the interior or 'outback' because of the arid conditions."

Rewrite the sentence with a word or two to complete a 5-W sentence in any order of the 5 W's.

_____

_____

_____

5. What is the order of 5 W's in the following sentence? "In the early 1800's, many English sought a new life in Australia because of a new breed of sheep called merinos." (*a*) where, what, who, why, when  (*b*) when, who, what, why, where  (*c*) when, who, what, where, why  (*d*) where, who, what, when, why

_____

6. List four features of Australia today that are mentioned in the selection.

_____

_____

## Comparison and Contrast; Cause and Effect

7. The best comparison of Australia during the 1700's to today would relate to (*a*) money  (*b*) geography  (*c*) cities  (*d*) farming.

_____

8. What is the major contrast between the population of Australia in the early 1800's and the late 1800's? Later there were more people who were  (*a*) wealthy (*b*) farmers  (*c*) sailors  (*d*) natives.

_____

9. What is a cause of the successful growth of the east coast?  (*a*) The Great Dividing Range  (*b*) merinos  (*c*) crocodiles and kangaroos  (*d*) "outback" conditions

_____

10. What effect did the discovery of gold in 1851 have on the population of Australia? (*a*) it created six colonies  (*b*) it doubled  (*c*) it tripled  (*d*) it had no effect

_____

## SOCIAL STUDIES PRACTICE C

**PREREADING**  Knowledge and understanding of major military conflicts is important. World War I was one such conflict that has affected both American and world history to the present.

Mankind has experienced conflict and war since the beginning of recorded history. World War I, however, ranks at the top of the most devastating of military hostilities with casualty tolls exceeding 10 million victims. In addition, shifted national alliances that resulted caused World War II and changed the course of history into the 21st century. The Great War was waged during the period of 1914–1918 and involved two groups of countries, the Allies and the Central Powers.

Serbian terrorist Gavrilo Princip assassinated Austria-Hungary's Archduke Francis Ferdinand on June 28, 1914, in Sarajevo to settle a vendetta between the two countries. This event sparked the war, but history had already been set in motion for eventual battle. First, many European nations experienced growing national pride followed by a significant buildup in military might. Also, these nations, desiring further colonization, formed new alliances with one another. Chief among the Allies were Britain, Italy, France, Russia, Serbia, and later, the United States. The Central Powers included Austria-Hungary, Bulgaria, Germany, and the Ottoman Empire.

Both sides waged bloody and catastrophic campaigns throughout these years on two geographic fronts. The Western Front ran along the borders of France and Belgium, while the Eastern Front occupied the borders of Russia and Austria-Hungary. In 1917 Russians experienced their own revolution and wanted a truce with the Central Powers. At the same time, America had remained neutral, but Germany was continually sinking unarmed ships. Americans decried this practice at home and abroad because of the loss of innocent life. In 1917 the United States joined the Allies and created an imbalance against the Central Powers.

In a January, 1918, address to Congress, President Woodrow Wilson named 14 points to be used as a guide for a peace settlement. On November 11, 1918, Germany finally surrendered and agreed to an armistice, thus ending World War I.

## Sequence

*1.* Before the start of World War I in 1914, what four events or conditions did European nations experience in sequence from the selection?

_____

_____

_____

_____

*2.* What is the sequence of events in the selection during 1917?  (*a*) Russian revolution, America enters the war, Germany sinks ships  (*b*) America enters war, Germany sinks ships, armistice signed  (*c*) America remains neutral, Germany sinks ships, America enters war  (*d*) America remains neutral, America enters war, Russian revolution

*3.* What is the sequence of events in the selection during 1918?  (*a*) peace plan, surrender, armistice, war ends  (*b*) surrender, armistice, peace plan, war ends  (*c*) surrender, war ends, peace plan, armistice  (*d*) peace plan, war ends, surrender, armistice

## 5 W's and Listing

4. Rewrite the first sentence of the second paragraph into the 5-W order of WHY, WHEN, WHO, WHAT, WHERE.

_____

_____

_____

5. The first sentence of the last paragraph contains 4 of the 5 W's. What are they in order of appearance?

_____

Now rewrite the sentence with a different order and add necessary information to include the missing 5th W.

_____

_____

_____

6. List the countries that belonged to the Allies and the countries that belonged to the Central Powers.

_____

_____

_____

_____

_____

_____

## Comparison and Contrast; Cause and Effect

7. What comparison can be made regarding mankind since the beginning of recorded history, according to the selection?

_____

8. Contrast the Western and Eastern Fronts with regard to location.

_____

9. What was the direct cause of the United States joining the Allies? (*a*) Russian revolution (*b*) Gavrilo Princip (*c*) Germans sinking ships (*d*) Fourteen Point Plan

_____

**10.** What effect did the United States' joining the Allies have on World War I?
(*a*) weakened Central Powers   (*b*) Germany sank more ships   (*c*) weakened Allies
(*d*) Russia joined Central Powers

---

## SCIENCE PRACTICE A

**PREREADING**   The polar bear is one of many species threatened with extinction because of our abusive intrusion into its habitats. Now it is time for us to assist this species in a healthy return to adequate numbers.

Above a glistening ice pack in the Bering Sea, a helicopter pilot stalks a polar bear, following paw prints in the snow. The bear suddenly appears as a hint of movement, white against white, padding its way across the ice. The helicopter descends, hovering over the frightened creature, and a shotgun slides out the window, firing a tranquilizer dart into a massive fur-covered rump. Minutes pass. The bear shows no effects. The helicopter drops for a second shot. This time the bear stands its ground, and the pilot, fearing the animal is about to lunge for the aircraft, abruptly noses the chopper skyward. He remembers how a 9-foot bear once swiped at a helicopter's skids, shredding the pontoons.

But this bear finally staggers, then stretches out on the ice like a giant sheepdog. The helicopter sets down, and the biologist Gerald Garner advances, poking the bear in the behind to make sure it is immobilized. A swivel of its head and a flashing of teeth warn Garner that there is plenty of defiance left in this 272-kg (600-lb.) carnivore. With a syringe, he injects more tranquilizer. At last, the head droops, and Garner can proceed. Around the bear's neck he fastens a vinyl collar containing a computer that will send data to a satellite, allowing scientists to keep track of the animal for a year. By the time Bear No. 6,886 raises its head, the helicopter is safely aloft . . .

Two decades ago, big-game hunters, not researchers, pursued polar bears from the air and on the ground, mostly for the prized fur. A thousand carcasses a year littered the Arctic. The number of ice bears dwindled, and there was a worldwide concern that the animal might be hunted to extinction. Today the bears' recovery is one of the success stories of conservation. Worldwide, polar bears now number at least 20,000, all of which are protected by a 1976 international agreement. Alaska has 3,000 to 5,000 polar bears, and only the state's Native Americans can hunt them—and strictly for subsistence purposes.

## *Sequence*

**1.** Which one of the following events occurs immediately after the helicopter drops for a second shot?   (*a*) the bear stands its ground   (*b*) the helicopter heads skyward   (*c*) the bear staggers   (*d*) the helicopter sets down

---

2. What is the last event in the selection regarding the biologist and the bear? (*a*) flashing of teeth   (*b*) biologist pokes the bear   (*c*) a collar is fastened (*d*) more tranquilizer is injected

3. How much time passes in the events of the first two paragraphs?   (*a*) about one hour   (*b*) about six hours   (*c*) about a day   (*d*) about a week

## 5 W's and Listing

4. What is the order of the W's in the first sentence of the selection?   (*a*) WHO, WHAT, WHERE   (*b*) WHEN, WHERE, WHAT   (*c*) WHERE, WHAT, WHO   (*d*) WHERE, WHO, WHAT

5. There are 5 W's in the first or topic sentence of the last paragraph. What is the order of these 5 W's?

    *When, who, what, why, where*

6. List three phrases that refer to the bear and its actions in the following sentence. "A swivel of its head and a flashing of teeth warn Garner that there is plenty of defiance left in this 272-kg (600-lb.) carnivore."

    *Swivel of its head, flashing its teeth, 272-kg carnivore.*

## Comparison and Contrast; Cause and Effect

7. How would you best compare the bear and its surroundings?   (*a*) both are cold (*b*) both have many visitors   (*c*) both are white   (*d*) both are tracked by satellites

8. Contrast the number of polar bears in the world and in Alaska.

    *5000*

9. What caused the helicopter to leave the area?   (*a*) the bear charged it   (*b*) hunters were approaching   (*c*) Gerald Garner was hurt   (*d*) the job was finished

10. What effect did the international agreement of 1976 have on polar bears? (*a*) increased worldwide hunting for food only   (*b*) less tracking   (*c*) more protection   (*d*) less conservation

## SCIENCE PRACTICE B

**PREREADING**   It is difficult to predict events without an understanding of the topic. Predicting the weather accurately is certainly one such topic.

Whether you are interested or not, there has to be weather. And it all happens in the section of the atmosphere called the troposphere. This section is about 6–10 miles above the surface of the earth. Meteorologists constantly study and chart conditions for many different reasons that affect life, property, and agriculture. Compared to the crude instruments and methods of folklore and yesteryear, today's scientists rely upon computers, radar, and satellites for observation and prediction.

Conditions on earth support life in contrast to other planets because of the relative balance of four conditions. These major conditions that affect weather are temperature, air pressure, wind, and moisture. The earth is heated by the sun, most of whose light and heat thankfully does not reach earth. But, that which does is absorbed and reflected by land and water. Most of this heat then radiates off the earth's surface and is absorbed back into the atmosphere where it is contained. This process keeps temperatures at levels necessary for plant and animal survival.

The atmosphere also exerts pressure on the earth's surface. Cool, dry air weighs more than moist, warm air which causes a higher pressure on the surface. Weather persons often refer to "highs" and "lows" during broadcasts or in newspapers. High pressure systems usually bring clear skies, while low pressure systems usually bring cloudy skies.

Wind is caused by temperature differences which then cause differences in air pressure. A high pressure always follows a low pressure. Wind speed increases or decreases according to pressure differences. Winds are nicknamed for the direction from which they blow, e.g. northerly, easterly, southerly, etc.

Moisture is the evaporation of water into the atmosphere, mostly from oceans but also from lakes, trees, and plants on land. Evaporation is caused by the sun's heat. Clouds form as a result of the liquid water evaporating into the gas called water vapor. This water vapor is carried upward by warm, rising air currents. Water vapor must adhere to any solid microscopic particle floating in the air. When water vapor cools enough, condensation takes place and a cloud forms. Once clouds cannot hold any more water vapor, the moisture is released. Rain results from temperatures above freezing above the earth and snow from temperatures below freezing.

Now take a look outside the window and think about whether you want to explain the weather patterns.

## *Sequence*

*1.* What is the correct sequence of pressure systems?   (*a*) low pressure follows high pressure   (*b*) high pressure follows low pressure   (*c*) high pressure follows easterly winds   (*d*) southerly winds follow pressure

2. What two events happen in sequence when water vapor cools enough?
(*a*) evaporation and rain   (*b*) high pressure and snow   (*c*) condensation and cloud formation   (*d*) none of these

_____

## 5 W's and Listing

3. Rewrite the following sentence by rearranging the W's and adding a "Why" of your own to complete the 5-W pattern. "Weather persons often refer to 'highs' and 'lows' during broadcasts or in newspapers."

_____

_____

_____

4. List the sources of evaporation from the selection.

_____

_____

## Comparison and Contrast; Cause and Effect

5. What would be the best comparison of cool, dry air and warm, moist air?
(*a*) both bring rain or snow   (*b*) both keep temperatures from changing
(*c*) both cause clouds to form   (*d*) both exert pressure on the earth

_____

6. What is the difference between the original amount of light and heat from the sun and that which reaches earth?   (*a*) less of both reach earth   (*b*) more light than heat reaches earth   (*c*) more heat than light reaches earth   (*d*) both reduce plant survival

_____

7. What causes earth to support life compared to other planets?   (*a*) proper prediction instruments   (*b*) a balance of four conditions   (*c*) methods of agriculture   (*d*) meteorologists

_____

8. What causes moisture?   (*a*) warm air   (*b*) clouds   (*c*) evaporation   (*d*) microscopic particles

_____

9. What effect does warm air have on water vapor?   (*a*) water vapor stays in water   (*b*) water vapor is carried upward to particles   (*c*) clouds cannot form   (*d*) high pressure forms

_____

10. What is the effect of evaporation, water vapor, and condensation?   (*a*) clouds and rain or snow   (*b*) high pressure and cloudy skies   (*c*) increased wind speed   (*d*) less heat reaches earth

_____

## SCIENCE PRACTICE C

**PREREADING**   America has a voracious appetite for energy to support its industry and the life-style of its citizens. How do we continue to provide energy demands required to continue this life-style into the 21st century?

As the light above provides the proper environment to read this article, think about the fuel, the cost, and the process of producing that light. Americans possess the heaviest appetite for energy and electricity in the world. The supply is not keeping up with this demand, which increases at an annual rate of 1%–2% with little regard for conservation.

Until the 1900's wood fulfilled the primary energy needs of the American home—cooking and heating. The turn of the 20th century witnessed the appearance of the automobile, electricity for mass use, and a booming industrial revolution. This technological advancement introduced coal followed by oil and then natural gas as the dominant fossil fuels to drive the home, car, and business. Throughout the history of fossil fuel use, however, came poisonous carbon dioxide emissions, dependence on foreign supplies, and the current "greenhouse effect" that is causing "global warming." Scientists thus looked to renewable energy sources such as water, the sun, and wind. But, while much cleaner and more available, the volume of production is limited, and the profit return for investors too little.

Enter the need to review the possibility of nuclear fission—the splitting of atoms to produce tremendous heat with which to make power. The United States has about 100 "nukes" that have struck fear in many minds and hearts. Clearly, nuclear power is a clean and cost-effective replacement for the fossils, but safety is the block to comfort. The radioactive waste materials of used nuclear fuel rods are strontium 90, cesium 137, and plutonium. No living form can escape the wrath of these deadly elements, if they enter earth, air, or water.

How and where to build totally safe nuclear reactors is a major question. How to convince investors and the public that accidents will not occur is a major question. Where to store radioactive waste for thousands of years is a major question. And, finally, how to reduce government red tape in granting permits and conducting hearings is a major question. Several nuclear accidents at home and abroad during the latter 1900's did little for public and government confidence. Perhaps French production of 75% nuclear power should be studied from both a public relations and scientific perspective.

Nuclear necessity may overrule option as the environment worsens from polluting fossil fuels, as electricity demand increases, and as politics becomes a major part of oil supplies for many countries. It may come down to a flick of the planning switch on the corporate and government walls to force new light on a major concern and need for the 21st century.

# Sequence

1. When were fossil fuels introduced for use?   (*a*) before the industrial revolution  (*b*) at the time of the industrial revolution   (*c*) after the industrial revolution  (*d*) after nuclear fission

2. Which of the following events followed the use of fossil fuels?   (*a*) carbon dioxide emissions   (*b*) global warming   (*c*) nuclear accidents   (*d*) all of these

3. What is the sequence of events during nuclear fission?   (*a*) atoms split, heat produced, power made   (*b*) heat produced, atoms split, power made   (*c*) atoms split, power made, heat produced   (*d*) none of these

# 5 W's and Listing

4. How many of the 5 W's are contained in the following sentence? "Americans possess the heaviest appetite for energy and electricity in the world."

   Rewrite the sentence with appropriate information to complete a 5-W pattern.

5. List the three waste materials of used nuclear fuel rods.

6. Use information from the fourth paragraph to write a 5-W sentence. Include the information in your answer to question 5.

# Comparison and Contrast; Cause and Effect

7. What would be the best comparison of nuclear energy to fossil fuels?   (*a*) more cost effective than renewable energy sources   (*b*) equal cause of the "greenhouse effect"   (*c*) equal government red tape   (*d*) dependence on foreign supplies

8. What would be the best contrast of fossil fuels to nuclear energy according to the selection?   (*a*) fossils are cleaner   (*b*) nuclear is cleaner   (*c*) nuclear reactors are outdated   (*d*) business wants nuclear

9. Use information from paragraph 4 to list three or more major causes for the lack of more nuclear power use in the United States today.

_____

_____

_____

10. Which of the following would be an effect of increased nuclear power in the United States? (*a*) less polluting fossil fuels (*b*) more investors in solar and wind (*c*) a declining environment (*d*) less demand for electricity

_____

## Thinking and Learning Activities
*Complete independently or in cooperative groups*

### WITHIN A SELECTION (SEE LANGUAGE ARTS PRACTICE C)

**1. Know**  List the five most important events in sequence from the beginning of the story to the conclusion in complete sentences with as many of the 5 W's as possible.
**2. Comprehend**  Retell the final paragraph as a news account on television with a short script including lists, 5 W's, and causes and effects.
**3. Apply**  Exhibit pictures of the characters in the selection from magazines, newspapers, etc.
**4. Analyze**  Compare and contrast the two or three least harmful events in the selection to the two or three most harmful events.
**5. Synthesize**  Contrive a list of the effects of the old man's giving Harrison the card.
**6. Evaluate**  Compare the actions of Harrison to what you would have done in the same circumstances.

### BEYOND A SELECTION (SEE SCIENCE PRACTICE B)

**1. Know**  Recall three severe weather conditions that you either read about or experienced or saw on television.
**2. Comprehend**  Restate a current weather forecast in your area using the newspaper or television with causes and effects.
**3. Apply**  Show a weather map from a newspaper and explain what is going on in your area.
**4. Analyze**  Compare and contrast the current weather in your area with weather in an opposite part of the United States, with another country in North or South America, and with a country of your choice in the world. Use cable weather reports or newspapers for your information.
**5. Synthesize**  Invent a new instrument for predicting weather. In paragraph form, give it a name, functions, and causes and effects of its functions on weather forecasting. Use some terminology from the selection in your description.

**6. Evaluate**   In a short paragraph, rate the importance of weather in your life using the 5 W's.

## ABOUT A SELECTION (SEE SOCIAL STUDIES PRACTICE C)

Use reference materials, movies, television programs, novels, and short stories to complete the following project.

1. Create a time line of the years 1914–1918. List two or three major events of World War I in sequence for each of these years with causes and effects for those events where possible.
2. Use the 5 W patterns to summarize in one paragraph each: a major battle of the war, a major personality from Europe, and a major personality from America, excluding President Wilson.
3. Compare and contrast maps of Europe in 1914 and today.
4. Watch the film, "All Quiet On The Western Front." Contrast the scenes in the film with those of your own life in two or three paragraphs.

# Unit IV   INTERPRETIVE CRITICAL THINKING SKILLS

## Overview the Skills

### 1. FACT OR OPINION

Facts are pieces of information that can be proved true because they are based on observations or measurements or studies. Opinions are statements that cannot be proved true, but are based on feelings or judgments.

When you read, you often have to distinguish between facts and opinions. When you write, you often use facts, or opinions, or both to inform or persuade.

Below are two columns. One is a list of facts and the other is a corresponding list of opinions related to the same topic. Read the lists and then explain how the facts could be proved true, while the opinions cannot be proved. When a sentence is part fact and part opinion, it is classified as an opinion.

*Facts*

1. China contains the highest population in the world.
2. Oceanography is a course required in grade 11.
3. Japan exports more cars than it imports.
4. President Johnson signed the Civil Rights Act in 1964.
5. Vaccines are available to prevent polio, a disease of the muscles.

6. Sir Arthur Conan Doyle created Sherlock Holmes, a detective, in Doyle's novels.

*Opinions*

China has the most problems in the world because of its population.

Oceanography is the most interesting course in grade 11.

Japanese cars are the choice of people around the world.

The Civil Rights Act of 1964 was the most crucial law of that year.

Vaccines are available to prevent polio, the most dreaded disease of the 20th century.

Sherlock homes was a good detective

7. _Panama canal_
   _was made in the_
   _1900's_

The construction of the Panama Canal in the early 1900's was the most impressive engineering feat of the 20th century.

8. _____
   _Cats are felines_   |   _cats have_
                        |   _many tricks._

For statement 6, fill in a corresponding opinion and for statement 7 a corresponding fact. Write a fact and related opinion of your own for statement 8 related to a science topic.

## On Your Own

In the parenthesis after each sentence, write *fact* or *opinion*. Then write a new fact or opinion of your own to show the opposite of your answer. The first sentence serves as an example.

1. Approximately 55,000 Americans lost their lives in the Vietnam War that was waged for ten years. (Fact)
   The Vietnam War brought the greatest waste of American lives in history and should never have lasted ten years.

2. Captains should never abandon their ships for any reason during any catastrophe. ( _Opinion_ )
   _captains should leave their ships_
   _so they can get a better one._

3. Earthquakes and their intensity are measured on a scale called the Richter Scale that gives an intensity reading from 0.1 through 10. ( _fact_ )
   _earthquakes are good things_
   _and bad at the same time._

4. Mark Twain was the pen name of Samuel Clemens who chose the pen name from "marking twain," a measurement of water depth on the Mississippi River. ( _fact_ )
   _mark twains name came_
   _from measuring the mississippi._

5. Losing the African elephant and Indian Bengal tiger to extinction would create another imbalance of nature that would prove most harmful to many other species' survival. ( _Opinion_ )
   _If the African elephant and_
   _Bengal tiger died out their ecosystems_
   _will adapt._

## 2. DRAWING CONCLUSIONS

The process of thinking goes hand in hand with all of your reading and writing. When you draw conclusions, you analyze topics, study characters, understand actions, sense feelings, and look at attitudes of the writer. You also learn about the mood or tone of the writing: does it make you happy, or sad, or angry?

As you begin to study and practice the critical thinking skills, remember that word *thinking*. You will not find all answers to questions specifically within a text. Drawing conclusions requires the use of text and your analysis of it to come up with answers to questions.

Read the following sentence and answer the questions that follow.

Operation Desert Storm was a test of the U.S.A.'s military strength against Iraq for several weeks in early 1991, as a result of Iraq's invasion of Kuwait in the Middle East during the latter part of 1990.

*1.* You would conclude that Operation Desert Storm was  (*a*) a medical accomplishment  (*b*) a peace treaty  (*c*) a war  (*d*) a novel.

_____

*2.* How many countries are mentioned in the sentence?  (*a*) 1  (*b*) 2  (*c*) 3 (*d*) 4

_____

*3.* Explain what is meant by the word *test* as used in the selection. a way to show something

*4.* How long ago did Operation Desert Storm take place? 20 years

## On Your Own

Read the three headlines from a newspaper below.

1. Plane Crash Casualties Reach 173 With More Expected
2. Europe Prepares For President's Visit
3. Daring Rescue Saves Two Boys On Icy Pond

Which one brings the most sadness? Why?
Which one brings happiness? Why?
Which one relates least to people? Why?
What is meant by the word *casualties*?

## 3. MAKING INFERENCES

As was the case with the previous skill of drawing conclusions, the skill of "making inferences" asks you to think about and analyze, in even more depth, what you are reading. Making inferences allows you to:

1. Expand vocabulary
2. Predict what might happen beyond the available information
3. Sense and describe mood, tone, or feelings
4. Clarify values
5. Draw comparisons and contrasts to information within a selection
6. Draw comparisons and contrasts to information in other selections

For example, suppose you were reading about the events of Black Thursday, the crash of the stock market on October 24, 1929. You would conclude that it started the Great Depression and caused President Hoover to lose reelection. But what inferences would you reach about the effect of the event on America's image in the world? What precautions are taken today to avoid a repeat of such events? What inferences would you reach concerning the emotions and experiences of unemployed people?

## On Your Own

Read the following paragraph and then answer the questions that follow.

Although international agreements are in effect, the supply of fish is declining. More countries are turning to the sea for these food sources, rich in nutrition and low in cost. The technology for catching fish with huge nets and larger fleets has outpaced nature's ability to replenish supplies. It would seem that balancing the needs of man and understanding the powers of nature need compromising.

*1.* What would you infer the international agreements relate to? (*a*) how much fish countries can catch. (*b*) what kinds of fish can be caught (*c*) where countries can fish (*d*) all of these

_____

*2.* What other technologies are available to increase fish catches other than those mentioned in the selection?

_____

_____

*3.* Give three inferences that you draw from the selection, if agreements are not followed.

_____

_____

_____

*4.* Copy the sentence that you infer contributes the most information to the problem.

_____

_____

5. The tone of the selection by the author is one of  (*a*) anger  (*b*) concern
   (*c*) indifference  (*d*) happiness
   Explain your answer _____

_____

## Practice the Skills

**PREREADING**   Poverty often forces people to give up some very personal pos-
sessions. How deep a sacrifice would you make?

> How much money would it take for you to part with one of your
> kidneys to save a life? Would you part with one for nothing? The human
> body can often function with one kidney.
>
> Each morning as the sun emerges above the horizon, thousands of
> poverty-ridden residents of Bombay, India, and the surrounding coun-
> tryside awaken to the hope of selling a kidney for profit. The daily scene
> since the late 1980's finds destitute people, desiring to be chosen, stand-
> ing in long lines outside donor clinics. It is a recurring scene in many of
> the larger cities. India is a country of severe indigence for a growing
> population of approximately 1 billion people. Extremely limited and un-
> sanitary water supplies plague the nation. Food preparation and provi-
> sions are also poor.
>
> Extreme overcrowding, poverty, unsanitary conditions, and polluted
> water and food supplies combine to create kidney failure among many
> of the people of India. It is a common cause of death across the popu-
> lation. However, only the wealthier can afford to purchase a kidney for
> potential survival. Thus, poor but healthy donors are selectively accepted
> at a clinic for a compensation of rupees equalling $1500 to $3000
> dollars paid upon successful surgery. Often, middleman brokers repre-
> senting needy recipients will seek out the most healthy and sound donors
> for private legal surgery.
>
> Rupees in the amount of hundreds or several thousands of dollars
> for one kidney can be a fortune in the eyes of the donor. Such a sum
> represents the amount earned over several years or even a decade of
> tedious labor on the streets or in factories for those fortunate to have
> employment. Donors use the kidney profit for many important reasons.
> Some pay off debt or buy a house. Pursuing a business venture is also a
> common use. Others purchase a television or radio or jewelry. Some
> families in India even apply money from a kidney sacrifice to the cost of
> a wedding. Any of these are worthwhile reasons for the forfeit of a body
> part in the mind of the donor.
>
> Of course, the health risks for both donor and recipient are great.
> About 20% of all donors die within a year as a result of disease in the
> remaining kidney. The ethical and moral questions of a society allowing
> such a practice are perhaps even greater. These questions relate to whether
> the government of India should allow its poorer citizens to engage in

life-threatening sacrifices for profit. Maybe more countries should follow India's lead and permit the donation of body parts for a price or even to the highest bidder. A kidney can save a life. So can a heart or lung. What should the policies be? How much is an organ or body part worth for profit or to provide the opportunity for continued life?

## Fact or Opinion

1. Which sentence in the first paragraph is a fact? (*a*) lst  (*b*) 2nd  (*c*) 3rd  (*d*) none of them

2. What is the order of fact-opinion for the first and last sentences of the fourth paragraph? (*a*) fact-opinion  (*b*) opinion-fact  (*c*) both are facts  (*d*) both are opinions

3. What is the order of fact-opinion for the following two sentences from the selection? "About 20% of all donors die within a year . . ." "Maybe other countries should follow India's lead . . ." (*a*) fact-opinion  (*b*) opinion-fact  (*c*) fact-fact  (*d*) opinion-opinion

## Drawing Conclusions

4. What is the major reason why Indians want to donate a kidney? (*a*) save lives  (*b*) make money  (*c*) improve medical services  (*d*) maintain population levels

5. What are middle-man brokers?

6. What is the greatest risk to a donor? (*a*) food poisoning  (*b*) loss of insurance  (*c*) death  (*d*) heart or lung disease

## Making Inferences

7. What is the ratio of donors to recipients? (*a*) more donors  (*b*) more recipients  (*c*) equal number of both  (*d*) not enough information to answer

8. Which of the following do you think best ranks the overall problems of India from most important to least important? (*a*) limited water supplies, kidney failure, overcrowding  (*b*) lack of housing, low wages, poor food preparation  (*c*) overcrowding, unsanitary conditions, poverty  (*d*) lack of businesses, unsanitary water, lack of home furnishings

**9.** Most people who donate a kidney place a high value on   (*a*) health   (*b*) education   (*c*) material goods   (*d*) retirement

---

**10.** How would you best describe the tone or feelings of the second paragraph for most readers of the selection?   (*a*) frustrating   (*b*) inspiring   (*c*) depressing   (*d*) uplifting
Explain your answer in one well-written sentence.

---

## Applying the Skills in Content Subjects

### LANGUAGE ARTS PRACTICE A

**PREREADING**   Tourist areas that once dotted the American countryside as little-known towns are now quite popular. Take a look at one such town and the reasons for its popularity and growth.

It is 200 miles south of Kansas City, near the center of the U.S. but isolated from everything. You reach it by a two-lane highway that snakes through the Ozark Mountains with nothing but oak trees for company. You round a corner and—*Look!*—there is a line of campers and cars stretching to the horizon, crawling along a five-mile strip of neon lights that flash from theaters, motels, and miniature golf courses.

Welcome to Branson, Mo. (pop. 3,706). This hardscrabble town attracts 5 million tourists a year, who drop an estimated $1.5 billion dollars into local pockets. And in a recession-slowed summer when many travelers are staying close to home and spending less, business in Branson is up 5% from last year.

The draw: big-time country-music shows, enough to fill 24 theaters every afternoon and evening, with stars such as Mickey Gilley, Loretta Lynn, Mel Tillis, and Reba McEntire, several of whom have moved to the area and own the theaters in which they perform. Nashville may still be the capital of country music, its recording and publishing hub, but Branson has become its Broadway. . .

Down-home hospitality keeps the audiences coming—mostly from a 300-mile radius that takes in St. Louis, Memphis and Wichita, but increasingly from all across the U.S. Patrons can meet the stars' families in theater lobbies; Tillis' wife, for one, sells candy. Most of the performers sit onstage at intermission to sign autographs, and violinist Shoji Tabuchi heads to the parking lot after his show to wave good-bye to the tour buses. Prices are right too. You can still get a motel room for $40, and there are 6,000 campsites in town. . .

Branson sees itself as a family attraction; almost every production has a flag-waving number. Some locals are less than thrilled by the heavy traffic. Many more jobs are available than in the past, but most are seasonal and pay at or near minimum wage . . . Mostly, though, the attitude is: "Don't bite the hand that feeds you."

But there is no turning back the clock. Too many tourists have found a friendly, affordable mecca in Branson; too many nationally known performers, some of whose hits are behind them, have found appreciative audiences. "It is an honest-to-goodness boomtown."

## Fact or Opinion

1. Copy the first sentence of the selection. Underline two phrases or parts of the sentence that are facts. Circle one phrase or part that is an opinion.

   _____

   _____

2. "Several . . . have moved to the area and own the theaters in which they perform."

   Is this a fact or opinion? _____ Now add information to create the opposite of your answer above.

   _____

   _____

3. How would you describe the fourth paragraph? (*a*) all facts (*b*) all opinions (*c*) mostly facts (*d*) mostly opinions

   _____

## Drawing Conclusions

4. What type of geography is not near Branson, Missouri? (*a*) ocean (*b*) forest (*c*) mountain (*d*) river

5. Which city competes with Branson for followers of country music? (*a*) St. Louis (*b*) Memphis (*c*) Wichita (*d*) Nashville

6. What word best replaces the word "mecca" as used in the selection? (*a*) performance (*b*) occupation (*c*) attraction (*d*) transportation

   _____

## Making Inferences

7. Which of the following would significantly expand the types of tourists and the number of visitors to Branson? (*a*) more famous stars (*b*) an airport (*c*) increased wages and jobs (*d*) more hotels

   _____

8. Rank the following reasons why you would visit Branson by arranging the letters in order of importance. Give one reason for your first answer. (*a*) hospitality (*b*) country music shows (*c*) cost (*d*) family attraction

_____

_____

9. You would most likely find the most information about Branson in a (*a*) music store (*b*) library (*c*) magazine (*d*) travel agency.

_____

10. Which statement best describes the attitude of most year-round residents of Branson, Missouri?
   a. There is a need for more stars, theaters, and hotels.
   b. Job opportunities should be limited to residents.
   c. Country music and followers bring problems, but let's not complain.
   d. Development of Branson should be slowed.

_____

## LANGUAGE ARTS PRACTICE B

**PREREADING** America has attracted immigrants since its settlement in the 1600's. For many immigrants the journey was, and still is, one of remarkable spirit.

Diep Tran was born in Saigon, South Vietnam, in 1975. He was the third son and youngest child of a clerk in the South Vietnamese Air Force and a housekeeper in a downtown hotel. It was the week in 1975 in which both Diep entered the world and the city of Saigon fell to communist rule, effectively ending the Vietnam War.

The next ten years brought discrimination at school for Diep, fourteen-hour workdays and seven-day workweeks for his parents, and deplorable housing and poverty for the Tran family. Diep's father died during that tenth year and one brother was imprisoned for some violation of government rules. One sultry, steaming, and stifling August night in that painful year, Diep's mother placed her son on a tiny boat with 114 strangers and kissed her son good-bye. The 115 modern day pilgrims were bound for America with little chance for fulfilling the journey.

The shock wore off and some of the pain of separation subsided, but Diep's suffering and misery were just beginning. Eight days of severely deficient food and water supplies, coupled with no sanitation conditions, ensued. The South China Sea provided merciful sailing conditions, but the August sun beat down upon the 96 survivors with relentless punishment. Each hour brought the prospect of a little more space for survival. Diep encouraged his new family to persevere.

On the ninth day, this bobbing mass of determined human spirit was rescued and brought to a Red Cross refugee camp in Thailand. Two months later, Diep Tran was united with cousins, aunt and uncle in a large east coast city of the United States to begin a new life. He spoke no English.

Eight years later, Diep Tran stood before his graduating high school class as valedictorian. With eyes brimming and voice breaking, Diep Tran epitomized the American dream for generations of past, present, and future immigrants. He related the good fortune of living in America to classmates and parents. He asked them to remember the many students in other parts of the world who live without opportunity. He invited all to join him in a future of hard work and goals to change the world for a better life. He especially thanked his family, both present and distant and past.

Weeping and cheering adults and classmates were images shadowed in Diep Tran's thoughts. Words and memories merged like the melodies of a church choir. He would forge these words and memories into an echo over the continents and across the South China Sea. If only to be heard and endeared by one special person.

## Fact or Opinion

*1.* How would you explain the fact-opinion content of the first paragraph? (*a*) all facts (*b*) all opinions (*c*) more facts than opinions (*d*) more opinions than facts

_____

*2.* Copy the only sentence in the second paragraph that is an opinion.

_____

_____

*3.* The following sentence is a fact. "Eight years later, Diep Tran stood before his graduating high school class as valedictorian." Rewrite the sentence into an opinion with necessary information changes.

_____

_____

_____

## Drawing Conclusions

*4.* Which of the following sets of conditions contributed the most difficulties during the journey? (*a*) number of travelers, heat, ocean conditions (*b*) lack of food and water, number of travelers, Thailand (*c*) no English spoken, ocean conditions, no sanitation facilities (*d*) number of travelers, heat, no sanitation facilities

_____

*5.* Choose two different words of your own to substitute for the word *persevere* as used in the selection.

_____

6. Diep Tran spent most of his first eight years in America concerned with (*a*) earning money (*b*) making friends (*c*) getting an education (*d*) doing volunteer service with the Red Cross.

## *Making Inferences*

7. You would infer that Diep's parents (*a*) supported communist rule (*b*) held better jobs than most relatives and friends after 1975 (*c*) understood opportunities in America (*d*) had family or friends in the transportation business.

8. What is meant by the sentence, "Each hour brought the prospect for a little more space for survival"? (*a*) rescue was near (*b*) people were dying (*c*) refugee camps were empty (*d*) none of these

9. What two qualities of character did Diep demonstrate during the journey and what other two qualities did he demonstrate up to graduation day?

10. In one or two sentences contrast the shift in feelings that you experienced from the first few paragraphs to the final few paragraphs.

## LANGUAGE ARTS PRACTICE C

**PREREADING** Prose and poetry are the only forms of written expression. How familiar are you with the structure and content of each?

The only two formal vehicles for written expression of thoughts, ideas, and feelings are prose and poetry. The author and the poet are polished artists who paint words onto a canvas of paper and bring beauty to language for the reader. The author creates prose in the structure of sentences and paragraphs. The poet creates poetry with a more complex makeup of structure and content.

The poet finely tunes language into a consistent structure of verse and stanza. A verse is one line of a poem and a stanza is a group of lines or verses. The verse may rhyme within a stanza or from one stanza to the next, which means that the poem has a rhyme scheme. Poetry does not have to rhyme; poems without rhyme are called blank verse.

It is the careful choice of words within this structure by the poet that enhances the meaning of a poem. Imagery is the technique of blending words into verse that appeals to the reader's or listener's emotions and the senses of sight, sound, taste, touch, or smell. The poet's objective, like that of the prose author, is to relate an experience, a feeling, and a meaning or message to the reader through language.

Following is a well-known poem by the famous American poet, Robert Frost. Read it for an understanding of its structure and meaning.

### STOPPING BY WOODS ON A SNOWY EVENING

Whose woods these are I think I know.
His house is in the village, though;
He will not see me stopping here
To watch his woods fill up with snow.

My little horse must think it queer
To stop without a farmhouse near
Between the woods and frozen lake
The darkest evening of the year.

He gives his harness bells a shake
To ask if there is some mistake.
The only other sound's the sweep
Of easy wind and downy flake.

The woods are lovely, dark, and deep,
But I have promises to keep,
And miles to go before I sleep,
And miles to go before I sleep.

It has been said that the gifted author or poet can "paint the color of the wind with words." The world's volume of prose and poetry, rich in structure and meaning, brings that gift to the appreciating reader or listener with each rustle of a turning page.

## Fact or Opinion

*1.* Copy two facts from the selection about the structure of poetry.

_____

_____

*2.* Which of the following lines from the poem by Robert Frost are opinions?
(*a*) 3, 9   (*b*) 1, 2   (*c*) 6, 7   (*d*) 5, 13

_____

3. Rewrite the following opinion from the selection into a fact. "Following is a well-known poem by the famous American poet, Robert Frost."

_____

_____

## Drawing Conclusions

4. The poem in the selection is an example of  (*a*) prose  (*b*) rhyme scheme  (*c*) blank verse  (*d*) none of these

_____

5. Line #8 in the poem, "The darkest evening of the year," is an example of  (*a*) verse  (*b*) stanza  (*c*) a feeling  (*d*) none of these.

_____

6. The selection compares authors and poets to  (*a*) sculptors  (*b*) painters  (*c*) teachers  (*d*) travelers. Explain the comparison.

_____

_____

## Making Inferences

7. A stanza and a poem are most like a  (*a*) driver and a car  (*b*) painter and a canvas  (*c*) paragraph and a story  (*d*) feeling and a meaning.

_____

8. The imagery of the poem in the selection appeals mostly to  (*a*) sight and sound  (*b*) sound and touch  (*c*) touch and smell  (*d*) sight and taste.

_____

9. Replace the last word in the last two lines of the poem with two separate sets of repeating words of your choice to maintain the meaning of the poem. (Rhyming with the first two lines is not necessary; thus your answers do not have to maintain any rhyming pattern.)

_____

_____

10. You would compare the tone and meaning of the poem by Frost to a personal experience such as a  (*a*) lunch break  (*b*) walk in the park  (*c*) dinner at a restaurant  (*d*) movie viewing

Explain _____

_____

What personal experience would contrast to the tone and meaning of the poem?

_____

## SOCIAL STUDIES PRACTICE A

**PREREADING**   Which of the 50 United States would you most like to visit? How about Wyoming?

Wyoming is a state of the United States that is famous for the beauty of its mountains. The peaks of the Rocky Mountains tower over the landscape. They provide the setting for the nation's largest and the world's oldest national park—Yellowstone. Wyoming also has the first national monument in the United States, Devils Tower, and the first national forest, Shoshone. Another famous scenic wonder, Grand Teton National Park, includes some of the West's most beautiful mountains. Millions of tourists visit Wyoming each year to enjoy its scenery and historic places.

Not all of Wyoming is mountainous. Between the mountain ranges in the state lie broad, flat, treeless basins. Some are dotted with rugged, lonely towers of rock called buttes. In the eastern part of the state, a flat, dry plain stretches westward toward the mountains.

Much of Wyoming's wealth comes from its land. About 50 percent of the state's land is used for grazing. Thousands of oil wells dot the prairies. Visitors may see a white-face steer cropping the grass near a pumping oil well. Petroleum, natural gas, coal, and other minerals make Wyoming an important mining state. Most of Wyoming's workers are employed in service industries. Service industries include such activities as education, health care, and retail trade.

The federal government owns almost half the land in Wyoming. Since the state depends mostly on its land, this makes the government especially important in Wyoming's economy. Federal agencies control grazing, logging, and mining activities that take place on the government land. The U.S. Air Force operates a nuclear missile base just outside Cheyenne, the state capital.

Wyoming has attracted travelers since the earliest days of white settlement. Three of the great pioneer trails cross Wyoming. The California, Mormon, and Oregon trails all took the covered wagons through South Pass. This pass became famous as the easiest way for the pioneers to travel across the mountains.

Millions of people have crossed Wyoming, but relatively few have stayed. The 1980 United States census reported that Wyoming had fewer people than any other state except Alaska. The 1990 census showed that Alaska had passed Wyoming, leaving Wyoming last among the states in population. Wyoming's largest city, Cheyenne, has only about 50,000 people.*

*Excerpted from *The World Book Encyclopedia.* © 1992 by World Book, Inc. By permission of the publisher.

## Fact or Opinion

1. Copy the phrase from the first sentence that makes it an opinion.

   _famous for its beauty_

2. Which of the following paragraphs is all facts? (*a*) 2nd (*b*) 3rd (*c*) 4th
   (*d*) 5th

   _____

3. Which one of the following best supports the last paragraph as being mostly facts?
   (*a*) interviews with people who crossed Wyoming (*b*) studies of Cheyenne,
   Wyoming (*c*) available census reports (*d*) government employment records

   _____

## Drawing Conclusions

4. Today people visit Wyoming primarily because of its (*a*) mountain passes
   (*b*) national parks (*c*) large cities (*d*) nuclear missile base.

   _____

5. In what direction would you be going if you wanted to travel across Wyoming
   from the mountains to the plains? (*a*) north to south (*b*) south to north
   (*c*) east to west (*d*) west to east

   _____

6. Which pair of words can be interchanged as used in the sentences of the selection?
   (*a*) government—agencies (*b*) industries—travelers (*c*) workers—pioneers
   (*d*) grazing—mining

   _____

## Making Inferences

7. What two industries exist together on most of Wyoming's land? (*a*) Air Force
   operations and retail trade (*b*) raising steer and health care (*c*) tourism and
   education (*d*) raising steer and mining

   _____

8. You would infer that most service industry jobs are located in (*a*) Cheyenne
   (*b*) Grand Teton (*c*) Yellowstone (*d*) U.S. Air Force base.

   _____

9. In one or two sentences, explain how Wyoming's geography contributed to early
   American history.

   _Wyoming had many trade_
   _routes to the coast._

   _____

**10.** Why have so many people crossed and visited Wyoming, but have relatively few stayed?  (*a*) people do not want to be near the missile base   (*b*) wages in most cities are low   (*c*) the government owns and controls much of the state's industries (*d*) Americans are eating less beef to support jobs in Wyoming

---

# SOCIAL STUDIES PRACTICE B

**PREREADING**   The Civil War tore the fabric of American society, 1861–1865. Much of the intensity of this conflict resulted from the contrasting contributions of two very different women.

No other issue in American history so divided opinion than the institution of slavery in the mid 1800's. The Confederate states and most people of the South held strongly to the right to own slaves to support the economy. The Union states and most people of the North held strongly to the abolition of slavery. It was this issue that most fueled the emotional and political fires that eventually split the country and kindled the Civil War, 1861–1865.

For ten years leading to the outbreak of war, a conflicting combination of personalities and events and circumstances were in force. The caldron in which these forces stewed contained two women. Their distinctly separate actions and accomplishments helped stoke the flames of fury that finally exploded on the battlefield in 1861, pitting American against American.

Etched into the annals of history are the chronicled and contrasting contributions of Harriet Beecher Stowe and Harriet Tubman. Each captured the tenor of the times as abolitionists during this tumultuous decade. Considering the dominance of government and society by men during this era, the influence on the war by two women rings even more loudly in Civil War discussions.

Writing was her forte and in 1852 Harriet Beecher Stowe, a white woman, penned the novel, *Uncle Tom's Cabin*. The book depicted the cruel and abused lives of slaves living lifetimes of labor on Southern plantations. Slave masters were cast in the role of inhumane treatment toward their subjects. These snapshots of Southern life created a scene of slavery that wrenched Northern emotions. For years an incensed South protested the novel's unfair portrayal of slavery, while the bitter feelings of the abolitionists swelled. After the Civil War President Abraham Lincoln said that Mrs. Stowe was "the little woman who wrote the book that made this great war."

Offering assistance to runaway slaves was her forte and throughout the 1850's Harriet Tubman, a black woman, was one leader of the "Underground Railroad." Despite a Northern law against assisting runaways to escape slavery, Tubman and this network of supporters moved slaves from place to place. These secret routes ran from the South to as far north as Canada. Freedom was the ultimate destination for those fortunate to succeed in using this imaginary railroad. Harriet Tubman assisted 300 slaves in their individual attempts to escape bondage. Large rewards were offered for Tubman's capture. But time and again she entered the South and risked her life for her fellowman.

Harriet Beecher Stowe and Harriet Tubman fanned the fires of contempt that each region of the United States held for the other in the years leading to 1861. While many personalities and factors create history, these two notable women have earned their place as stars in the constellation of American history.

## Fact or Opinion

1. How would you describe the first paragraph?  (*a*) all facts  (*b*) all opinions  (*c*) mostly facts  (*d*) mostly opinions

2. Rewrite the following fact into an opinion. "Writing was her forte and in 1852 Harriet Beecher Stowe, a white woman, penned the novel *Uncle Tom's Cabin.*"

3. What phrase from the quote by President Lincoln makes the sentence an opinion?  (*a*) the little woman  (*b*) who wrote the book  (*c*) that made this great war  (*d*) all phrases are opinions

## Drawing Conclusions

4. How many years have passed since the end of the Civil War?

5. Which one of the following is not a topic in *Uncle Tom's Cabin* as discussed in this selection?  (*a*) slave life  (*b*) slave labor  (*c*) slave escape  (*d*) slave masters

6. Choose the pair of words that best replaces the pair of italicized words in the following sentence from the selection. "These *snapshots* of Southern life created a scene of slavery that *wrenched* Northern emotions."  (*a*) images—upset  (*b*) pictures—lessened  (*c*) ideas—destroyed  (*d*) books—satisfied

## Making Inferences

7. What effect did Harriet Beecher Stowe's book have on both the North and the South?  (*a*) it upset the South more than the North  (*b*) it upset the North more than the South  (*c*) it upset both equally  (*d*) it didn't upset either

*8.* Who probably offered the rewards for Harriet Tubman's capture? (*a*) abolitionists (*b*) slaves who could not escape (*c*) plantation owners (*d*) Canadians

---

*9.* Why was the Civil War such a significant event in American history? (*a*) *Uncle Tom's Cabin* would not have been written (*b*) American fought against American (*c*) President Lincoln was elected as a result of the war (*d*) Harriet Tubman helped to form the Underground Railroad

---

*10.* Explain the author's use of the words "stars" and "constellation" in the final sentence of the selection.

---

---

---

---

## SOCIAL STUDIES PRACTICE C

**PREREADING** The right to vote is granted in the Constitution. Should citizens be required to exercise this right?

Like the crumbling walls of a dynamited building, the once formidable number of totalitarian and communist governments around the world might well be diminishing into history. Historians may study the crossroads of the 20th and 21st centuries as wonderful testimony to the will and strength of oppressed peoples. This era may reveal democracy as the ignition charge that leveled these despotic governments. Clearing the rubble for new world direction may be the bulldozers of democracy and the possible construction of new governments "of the people, by the people, and for the people." It may have been freedom and the right to vote that most inspired the vigor and sustained the momentum to status as a newly independent nation. Are these facts or opinions? History will give the answers.

America, however, has experienced such status since 1776. Through today, America has been the portrait of democracy in the museum of nations, a picture of life sought and modeled by many countries. But America now faces a wake-up call. Isn't it time to improve the United States' record of voter registration? Isn't it time to show the world that all Americans respect independence and participate in the electoral process? Isn't it time to establish an image in which 100% of American citizens over the age of eighteen are registered to vote and nearly that number perform their civic duty on election days?

Approximately 75 million, or one half of the eligible voters in America, are not even registered to vote! Approximately one quarter to one half of those who are registered do not vote on most election days! These facts mean that many candidates for public office at the local, state, and federal levels are elected by about one quarter, or one out of four, of adult Americans! A 1983 comparison study showed that the U.S. had the lowest rate of voter participation in federal elections among 23 democratic nations!

The reasons for these distressing figures range from citizen apathy to distrust for politicians to complicated registration rules and schedules. Federal and state agencies are attempting to streamline the registration process. Endeavors to increase eligible voters include registration with driver's license renewal, registration by mail, and keeping registration status with a change of address.

Of course, more registered voters may not equal more participating voters. While some Americans believe that not registering and not voting are also rights, it does ring a hollow and haunting echo to "government of the people, by the people, and for the people." Don't forget the causes and reasons for all of those authoritarian governments in the first place. Isn't it time to wake up, America?

## Fact or Opinion

*1.* Copy the only sentence in paragraph 2 that is a fact.

_____

_____

*2.* Are the figures, statistics, and sources cited in paragraph 3 facts, or opinions?

_____

*3.* How would you describe paragraphs 1, 2, 4, and 5?  (*a*) mostly facts  (*b*) mostly opinions  (*c*) a balance of both fact and opinion  (*d*) none of these

_____

## Drawing Conclusions

*4.* The phrase "electoral process" as used in the selection relates to  (*a*) communist rule  (*b*) independence  (*c*) voting  (*d*) driver's license.

_____

*5.* Copy the entire sentence from the selection that has the information to answer the following question. How do Americans compare in voting to other countries with the right to vote?

_____

_____

*6.* You would conclude from the recommendations to increase voter registration that many Americans often  (*a*) change address  (*b*) do not renew driver's license  (*c*) do not read their mail  (*d*) none of these.

_____

## Making Inferences

7. What is the overall concern of the author? (*a*) too many countries are communist (*b*) politicians need to be trustworthy (*c*) not enough candidates run for public office (*d*) not enough Americans vote

   _____

8. What minimum range of percent of support from the adult Americans on election day would almost assure election of a candidate for office? (*a*) 20–40% (*b*) 40–60% (*c*) 60–80% (*d*) 80–100%

   _____

9. You would infer that the author wants America to "wake up" in order to (*a*) bring a decline in authoritarian governments (*b*) reduce the voting registration requirements (*c*) get people to vote and preserve American ideals (*d*) reduce the legal voting age to increase the number of voters.

   _____

10. You would most likely find this selection in a(n) (*a*) short-story book (*b*) editorial page (*c*) history textbook (*d*) construction manual Explain your answer in one well-written sentence.

    _____

    _____

    _____

## SCIENCE PRACTICE A

**PREREADING**  How much do you know about the habit of cigarette smoking?

No butts about it—take a healthy stroll along any beach, sidewalk or shopping mall. Observations will always reveal the shortened, flattened, and shredded evidence of addiction. An average of 1 in 3 Americans over 18 inhales many harmful chemicals (many are cancer causing) from the average of 200 packs or 4,000 cigarettes smoked annually. And this number of smokers does not include a startling number of younger Americans under 18 who engage in the habit. This personal pollutant costs hundreds or thousands of dollars a year and tens of thousands of dollars over the lifetime of a smoker. Certainly, there are better ways to spend hard earned dollars by all of these people.

Let's filter out a few more smoldering statistics related to this health hazard. About one-half million Americans die each year of cancer. One-third of these deaths are smoking related, as shown in medical studies. One of every four cancers is in the lung and studies prove that nearly all lung cancer victims have some history of smoking. Smokers are nearly ten times more likely than nonsmokers to die from lung cancer. Only 10% of all lung-cancer patients survive beyond five years of diagnosis. Cancers of the larynx, mouth, and esophagus are also linked to smoking. Clearly, smoking causes cancer for each addicted smoker.

A pack of other diseases and health concerns can also be related to these puffing and protruding perils of the lips. Bronchitis and emphysema often plague the smoker and create great breathing problems. Colds are more commonly experienced by the smoker. Studies also indicate a direct link between smoking and heart disease, the leading killer of Americans. Blood vessels constrict, blood pressure increases, and the heart pumps harder in the body of a smoker. Also, chemical-laden smoke impedes the amount of oxygen carried throughout the body by red blood cells. Reducing normal oxygen supply diminishes organ function over a long period of time. Finally, babies born to smokers are smaller on the average, while maternal smoking slightly increases the chance for fetal or early infant death. Indeed, is smoking worth these health risks?

Of course, the tobacco industry gives a carton of reasons why people should smoke. There must be some success, because the companies realize sales of about 30 billion dollars each year. Aggressive advertising, no longer allowed on television, encourages the men, women, and children of America to smoke. The image and message of most ads is that smoking is a socially mature and sophisticated habit. Blend in the contrasting attitudes and actions of nonsmokers, people subjected to passive smoke, and health and government officials. The results are lawsuits, laws banning smoking in public places, and active advertising campaigns against smoking. Naturally, the entire issue generates fuming attitudes on both sides of the question.

No "butts" about it—to smoke or not to smoke is a burning question of life and breath that equally affects all Americans. Don't forget those crumpled remnants and reminders of the habit that litter our every surrounding. Surely, the issue of smoking is and should continue to be a primary national concern.

## *Fact or Opinion*

*1.* List three statistical facts from the selection.

_____

_____

_____

*2.* What are the concluding sentences in each paragraph?   (*a*) all facts   (*b*) all opinions   (*c*) mostly facts   (*d*) mostly opinions

_____

3. Do you think that the tobacco industry and its advertising deals mostly with facts, or opinions? Explain your answer.

_____

_____

_____

_____

## Drawing Conclusions

4. What would be the cost of smoking one pack per day at two dollars per pack for forty years?

_____

5. Smoking-related diseases and deaths will most often be those of   (*a*) lung cancer or mouth cancer   (*b*) emphysema or bronchitis   (*c*) lung cancer or heart disease   (*d*) heart disease or fetal death.

_____

6. What do you think is meant by "passive smoke"?

_____

_____

## Making Inferences

7. The author is concerned about the effects of smoking on what particular group of people?   (*a*) the unborn and infants   (*b*) Americans under 18   (*c*) the elderly   (*d*) all of these

_____

8. Why would tobacco companies direct smoking advertising toward Americans under 18?

_____

_____

9. What is a major problem in reducing the amount of smoking in America?
   (*a*) fewer lawsuits   (*b*) more advertisements against smoking   (*c*) loss of jobs in the tobacco and advertising industries   (*d*) more available smoke-free public places

_____

**10.** Copy five sentences from the selection in order of importance that might prevent you from beginning smoking or cause you to quit the habit.

_____

_____

_____

_____

_____

_____

_____

_____

_____

_____

## SCIENCE PRACTICE B

**PREREADING**   The world is losing species of plant and animal life at an alarming rate. The problem equally applies to America and requires action.

Benjamin Franklin nominated the wild turkey as the symbolic bird of America. However, it was the bald eagle, awe-inspiring and majestic in flight, that became the national bird. It was the best choice to show the right image of a young America. But today the bald eagle, unlike the wild turkey, perches on the edge of extinction in the lower 48 states. This is true despite federal protection since 1940. Joining the hundreds of other plants and animals, the eagle now symbolizes a vigorous conservation effort.

This effort reaches out to the three categories of wildlife that need consistent attention. The "extinct," the "endangered," and the "threatened" species of plant and animal life have begun to receive priority attention. The Endangered Species Act was passed in 1973. It was the most important government act of that decade. Protection of natural habitats and pollution controls were enacted through this law. Its primary objective was the restoration of healthy populations of plants and animals facing extinction in the 50 United States. The law, however, was only a beginning.

Natural conditions contributed much to species loss throughout primitive history. The Ice Age, disease, and inadequate food supplies may be blamed for the loss of the dinosaur, the saber-toothed tiger, the mastodon, and other plants and animals thousands of years ago. But recent history exposes man as the primary cause of extinct and declining species. Today, it is pollution and pesticides that pose the threat. Further, add overpopulation, expanding farmlands, highway and dam construction, forest depletion, and illegal hunting as other dangers to preserving wildlife. Then include the factors of politics and the economic needs of business expansion for jobs. The problem of balancing and protecting the environment becomes very complex.

Interest groups and ecologists believe that the government maintains a less than sincere commitment to preserving wildlife and sides with business too much, despite the 1973 law. Federal authorities point to more recent clean air and water acts, strict hunting and fishing laws, regulated national parks, and the purchase of land tracts for wildlife refuges as proof of their commitment. All Americans are more conscious of the environment. However, more action is needed to preserve species.

Where is the balance of need struck? Grizzly bears, Florida panthers, and eastern timber wolves need to know. So do the California condor and the whooping crane. Add the Houston toad, the snail darter fish, and the Hawaiian kokla cookei plant to this growing list of life teetering on the edge of extinction. And the list of extinct or endangered American species is significantly less in comparison to that of many other countries around the world.

Man's need for nature has always been clear. What is nature's need for man? Which one could survive without the other? Hopefully, the needs of both will balance comfortably on the wings of soaring eagles for generations to come.

## Fact or Opinion

*1.* Which of the following sentences in the first paragraph are both facts?   (***a***) 1, 3 (***b***) 4, 5   (***c***) 5, 6   (***d***) 1, 6

_____

*2.* What phrase in the second sentence of the first paragraph makes it an opinion?

_____

_____

*3.* Explain why paragraph 4 is a complete set of opinions.

_____

_____

## Drawing Conclusions

*4.* Who or what did NOT contribute to the loss of the saber-toothed tiger according to the selection?   (***a***) weather   (***b***) man   (***c***) disease   (***d***) inadequate food supplies

_____

5. You would conclude that the Endangered Species Act   (*a*) saved the bald eagle (*b*) established pollution controls   (*c*) caused a decline in interest groups (*d*) helped business interests.

_____

6. What are whooping cranes and snail darters?   (*a*) extinct species   (*b*) endangered species   (*c*) unthreatened species   (*d*) none of these categories

_____

## *Inference*

7. You would infer from the entire selection that which of the following is most needed to preserve wildlife?   (*a*) strict hunting laws   (*b*) national parks (*c*) clean air and water   (*d*) less business interest in wildlife

_____

8. Which group has contributed the most to wildlife preservation?   (*a*) government officials   (*b*) interest groups   (*c*) average Americans   (*d*) business people Explain your answer.

_____

_____

9. Aside from possible extinction in the lower 48 states, why is it so necessary to preserve the bald eagle?

_____

_____

10. Answer the two questions in the final paragraph with one reason to support each answer.

_____

_____

_____

_____

### SCIENCE PRACTICE C

**PREREADING**   Information about an individual's blood and tissue type can save the life of a total stranger many miles away. How should such a need be organized and who should assume such a responsibility, if at all?

> My brother Paul and I took only one walk together in the summer of 1984. He had leukemia. Doctors gave him a 20 percent chance of living more than a year. The sun was shining and our steps were strong. "Why are you so upbeat?" I asked.
> He smiled. "We'll transplant bone marrow, and I'll be saved," he said. Paul was a doctor, on staff at one of America's best hospitals, and

I listened carefully as he explained how marrow from our sister, Joby, or me might save him. Later that week, technicians took our blood and we tried to keep busy while waiting for test results. When the telephone rang, it was bad news because neither of us matched Paul. In less than eight months, he was dead.

Several years later I read about a woman in Wisconsin who gave marrow—and life—to a six-year-old girl in North Carolina. A new donor registry brought them together. This prompted me to study what could be accomplished with registries. In America alone, as many as 13,000 strangers might have saved my brother—if society had established mechanisms to find them.

But the more I saw, the more I came to realize that the story is much larger than linking donor and recipient. It extends deeply into what binds us together. Donated organs and tissues give life and sight, teach researchers how the brain works, provide drugs for fighting cancer, and allow us to master the very genes that define us as human.

Even small gifts can become miracles. Transplantation of dopamine-producing cells into the brain can reduce symptoms of Parkinson's disease, and the injection of immature muscle cells can give renewed strength to diseased muscles. Insulin producing islet cells may cure diabetes, which kills tens of thousands of people each year.

If you save one life, the Talmud teaches, you save the world. By using donated material to harness commonality among all human cells and genes, medical technology has given this new meaning. Each of us, while we live and after we die, may now save the world many times over. We may also help future generations in ways the wisest among us cannot yet imagine. This medical revolution affects everyone, yet it is emerging quietly, in a series of little-noticed struggles.

## Fact or Opinion

*1.* Underline the phrase in the following sentence that makes it an opinion. "Paul was a doctor, on staff at one of America's best hospitals, and I listened carefully as he explained how marrow from our sister, Joby, or me might save him."

*2.* List three medical facts from the selection.

_____

_____

_____

*3.* Copy a fact that brings sadness.

_____

_____

Copy an opinion that is uplifting.

_____

_____

## Drawing Conclusions

**4.** Which of the following is NOT a part of donor programs in this selection? (***a***) allows more research   (***b***) provides profits for donors   (***c***) provides drugs for patients   (***d***) saves lives

**5.** What is the job of "registries"?   (***a***) provide shelter for leukemia patients and their families   (***b***) store donated organs   (***c***) store donor and recipient information   (***d***) treat Parkinson's disease and diabetes

**6.** Explain how the word "gifts" is used in the sentence from the selection: "Even small gifts can become miracles."

## Inferences

**7.** You would infer that the family most needed what kind of strength to get through the experiences in the introductory paragraphs?   (***a***) emotional   (***b***) physical (***c***) financial   (***d***) social

**8.** What is the Talmud?   (***a***) a hospital   (***b***) a research team   (***c***) a technology (***d***) a collection of writings

**9.** Explain the sentence "Each of us, while we live and after we die, may now save the world many times over."

**10.** How would you describe the transition of tone and feelings in the selection from the beginning to the conclusion?   (***a***) sadness to happiness   (***b***) anger to sadness (***c***) sadness to hopefulness   (***d***) depression to concern

## Thinking and Learning Activities

*Complete independently or in cooperative groups*

### WITHIN A SELECTION

**1. Know**   (See Social Studies Practice B.) Relate information from the selection that you learned about the Civil War in the following form and in complete sentences. The first is a sample.

First, I learned that the Southern states were called the Confederacy and believed in slavery, while the Northern states were called the Union and believed in the abolition of slavery.

Second, I learned

Then, I learned

Finally, I learned

**2. Comprehend** (See Science Practice A.) Review the information in the selection and fill in the K-W-L model of understanding what you read with four more pieces of information in each column. A sample entry for each column is provided.

| K | W | L |
|---|---|---|
| What I **know** | What I **want** to find out | What I **learned** and still need to know |
| 1. many Americans smoke cigarettes | 1. how many people under 18 smoke | 1. what are the chances of getting cancer if you quit |

**3. Apply** (See Social Studies Practice C.) Apply vocabulary words of your own to replace words in the selection.

Copy five sentences from the selection with at least two or more words that are challenging in meaning. Underline two or more words of your choice in each sentence and write a replacement word of your own above each underlined word.

**4. Analyze** (See Social Studies Practice B.) Compare and contrast the contributions of Harriet Beecher Stowe and Harriet Tubman in one paragraph. Then, in a second paragraph, explain which woman's contribution was more important to the overall history of the Civil War and American history. Give reasons for your position.

**5. Synthesize** (See Language Arts Practice B.) Arrange Diep Tran's nine days at sea into a diary of facts and opinions of events, sights, and feelings. Each day's entry should be in well-written sentences.

**6. Evaluate** (See "Practice the Skills.") Decide whether the government of India should ban the practice of allowing citizens to donate kidneys for profit. Give your reasons in a well-written paragraph of 4–7 sentences with a balance of facts and opinions.

## BEYOND A SELECTION

**1. Know** (See Language Arts Practice C.) Name the titles of three stories and three poems that you have read and enjoyed.

**2. Comprehend** (See Language Arts Practice A.) Locate an article from a newspaper or magazine that refers to vacation destinations. Copy two facts and two opinions from the article. Then rewrite the sentences into new opinions for the facts and new facts for the opinions.

**3. Apply** (See Social Studies Practice B.) Exhibit a picture of an American woman who made a contribution to American history like that of Harriet Beecher Stowe or Harriet Tubman. Explain the choice and the contribution in one well-written paragraph.

**4. Analyze** (See Social Studies Practice C.) Survey ten adults over 18. Ask the following questions and chart the answers. 1) Are you registered to vote? 2) Do you vote on most election days? 3) What is the main reason why you do vote? *or* What is the main reason why you don't vote?

What conclusions do you draw from the poll compared to the information in the selection?

**5. Synthesize** (See Science Practice B.) Imagine that you could have the power to preserve all of wildlife, but in so doing many, many jobs would be lost and the economy of America would suffer. Or, suppose that you could develop business interests and create many, many good jobs, but much wildlife would become extinct.

Explain your choice in one well-written paragraph with both facts and opinions.

**6. Evaluate** (See Science Practice C.) Choose a story or novel or television program or movie. Compare the feelings you had about your choice with the feelings you had while reading this selection.

## ABOUT A SELECTION

Use appropriate selections in this unit to develop information for well-written paragraph answers. You may also use other print or nonprint materials such as maps, pictures, or television to assist you in answering the questions.

1. Give 3–5 comparisons of Language Arts Practice A and Social Studies Practice A. Then, in a second paragraph, give 3–5 contrasts between the two selections.

2. Social Studies Practice C and Science Practice A both show a concern. Which selection and its concern do you think impact American society more today? Support your answer with as many good reasons as possible.

3. Refer to Language Arts Practice B and predict 5–10 events in Diep Tran's life during the year after his graduation with emphasis on student experiences and expectations.

4. Write a one paragraph piece of prose that makes the reader happy. Write an eight-verse, two-stanza poem that makes the reader sad. Have the topic for each relate to a selection in this unit. Refer to Language Arts Practice C for appropriate use.

5. In a first paragraph, explain three comparisons in medicine and donor programs as shown in Practice the Skills and in Science Practice C. In a second paragraph, give three contrasts.

# Unit V  HIGHER ORDER CRITICAL THINKING SKILLS

## Overview the Skills

Author's Introductory Note: In questions and activities dealing with Higher Order Critical Thinking Skills, answers or responses may not always be clear-cut. Some of the answers or responses are not necessarily "right" or "wrong," but rather are "better" or "best." Even in questions with multiple-choice answers, some are better than others while few are simply wrong.

## 1. REASONING

In the previous unit you learned about drawing conclusions and inferences, skills that require you to think about and understand information in order to arrive at answers to questions. The skill of "reasoning" takes these steps of thinking and understanding one important step further.

Reasoning involves analyzing not only the new information before you, but also including knowledge that you already have. Often, your past experiences enter this thinking and analyzing and problem-solving process. For example, laws in some states require all motorcycle and mo-ped riders to wear a helmet. How does your own experience or that of someone you know shape your opinion of this law?

a. Should the law be extended to bicycle riders? What about skateboarders? And roller skaters, especially single-blade?
b. Should there be fines for noncompliance?
c. What amounts and what process for collection should be enforced for such fines?
d. How should the money for collected fines be used?

The mature reader and writer draws from all skills to analyze and understand information from text and experience to broaden the learning process. It will also improve your writing and improve your performance on tests.

### On Your Own

Read and think about the following issue. Then write possible answers to the questions that follow.

A law requiring seat belts (worn by all passengers) and air bags be mandatory equipment in all vehicles.

1. What agencies should monitor the enforcement of wearing seat belts and the operating condition of air bags?

_____

_____

2. Who should be liable for malfunctioning air bags in which a serious injury or death results?

_____

_____

3. How could air bags be installed as a safety device for rear-end or side collisions? Should these also be mandatory?

_____

_____

## 2. THEME

Theme is what the selection, story, novel, movie, or anything studied in length is really all about in one or two words. Again, you will have to employ thinking and analysis to come up with the theme. Sometimes, the theme word(s) appears within the selection. Also, it is a good idea to have a thesaurus during the analysis of theme for alternative words that may serve as more exact theme words.

Remember the novel *White Fang*. True, the story is about a boy and a wolf, but the theme is companionship or devotion. How about the movie *E.T.* The theme was friendship between Elliot and E.T. and the theme of courage enters as E.T. is helped during the escape. The theme might be perseverance in a story of a girl who grows up in poverty and goes on to become a doctor or lawyer. The theme of jealousy might be the backdrop of a story of one friend's attempt to cause hardship for the other. Shakespeare's plays often reflect the themes of envy, greed, prejudice, conflict, or loyalty.

Themes are important because they develop a very deep understanding of what you read or view or experience. These understandings expand your abilities at school and at work.

### On Your Own

Refer to the selections in Unit IV that you just completed to answer the following.
1. The theme of the Practice the Skills selection might be "sacrifice."
2. The theme of Language Arts Practice A might be  (*a*) amusement  (*b*) competition  (*c*) conflict  (*d*) tourism.

_____

3. The theme of Language Arts Practice B might be   (*a*) fear   (*b*) survival   (*c*) perseverance   (*d*) destruction.

_____

4. The theme of Social Studies Practice B might be   (*a*) conflict and sacrifice   (*b*) politics and profits   (*c*) inequality and unemployment   (*d*) competition and women's liberation.

_____

5. What are the themes of the three Science Practices A, B, C, in Unit IV?

_____

_____

_____

## 3. AUTHOR'S PURPOSE OR BIAS

The author always has a "purpose" for what he or she writes. The purpose may be to instruct or to narrate events or to describe or, most often, to persuade the reader to accept a position on a topic. It is your job when you read to decide on the author's purpose, because this understanding will further develop comprehension and critical thinking skills.

As a reader with critical thinking skills, you should also understand the need to recognize the author's "bias." Bias refers to the attitude the author has toward the people or topics in the writing. An author may take a position on a subject wanting to get support from the reader for that position. This "siding" on a particular issue is also bias.

For example, a nutritionist may try to persuade readers to improve health by changing their diet from processed foods to natural foods. Or a coach of a football team might write a conditioning guide stressing weight lifting, while a track coach would stress running and aerobic exercise.

Sometimes, the bias is brought out through sarcasm, seriousness, humor, or praise. Author's purpose and bias are also related to the mood or tone of the writing. All of these skills are part of writing and require you to understand how they function to help you become a mature reader and writer.

Read the following passage and think about author's purpose and bias as well as the mood and tone of the writing.

Did you ever consider why so many people are afraid of wolves and spiders? There is a simple answer to this question that places so many people in the category of canus lupus phobics and/or arachnophobics. Just think about all the negative exposure to wolves and spiders we received as children from two little tales. Yes, "The Three Little Pigs" and "Little Miss Muffet" did little to establish a fond impression of these creatures. What if the wolf saved the pigs from a mean old farmer or Miss Muffet was in the habit of catching spiders for medical research and tortured the little spindly insects on a regular basis? Along comes one and evens the score with Miss Muffet. You can't make these kinds of impressions on little kids and then expect support for nature's creatures from these kids as adults.

## On Your Own

Think about and answer the following questions about the passage you have just read.

*1.* What is the author's purpose in writing this?

_____

_____

*2.* Does the author have a legitimate point to make? _____

*3.* What is the author's bias?

_____

_____

*4.* How would you describe the mood or tone of the selection?

_____

## Practice the Skills

**PREREADING**   In the early days of television during the 1950's, children often carried their lunches to school in tin lunch boxes. Often, a favorite television character or hero would be colorfully painted on the lunch box. What values did those characters represent during that American era?

Let's bring those lunch box heroes back for an encore! Entombed in the cinema and videotape archives rest hundreds of characters and thousands of episodes that inculcated millions of American children with a lifetime of values. The advent of television revolutionized entertainment and brought an array of personalities into the American living room, beginning in the 1950's. A new world of figures emerged with morals and values and a portrait of American history that may never again grace the American image and life-style.

They may have lived an abbreviated screen life, but audiences of millions viewed their performances, admired their presence and actions, and carried the lunch box of a favorite hero to school each day. Who were some of these lunch box heroes?

The influence of the West in American history brought two famous frontiersmen to the screen some two centuries after their actual roles in history. Daniel Boone and Davy Crockett were household names in the early era of television. Crockett was by far the more adored. With the coonskin cap as his trademark, he epitomized fair play and actively supported the rights of the native American Indian during his life all the way to election to the U.S. House of Representatives and back home to Tennessee. Davy Crockett symbolized rugged individualism and the frontier spirit. Those who followed his weekly encounters with grizzly bears and marauders will never forget the Davy Crockett jingle and his legacy as "king of the wild frontier."

The legacy of the American cowboy kept hats, cap guns, and string ties in vogue throughout the 50's. Riding across the screen and depicting values of honesty, decency, and loyalty were several memorable cowboys and cowgirls. Hopalong Cassidy paved the way. Equal to the task of representing the West was Annie Oakley, a for-real cowgirl brought to life on the screen from the personality who traveled with the Wild West Show of Buffalo Bill Cody in the mid-1800's. But the most famous keeper of television law and order within the cowboy genre had to be the Lone Ranger and his trusted, loyal partner, Tonto. No two TV figures were closer friends. No viewer ever watched an episode without hoping for the Lone Ranger's mask to dislodge for a peek at his true identity.

As the television industry expanded its genres, supernatural characters were reincarnated from the comic book to the screen. Wonder Woman and, especially, Superman provided weekly protection for the forces of good against the forces of evil. Superman's legacy will always be the tireless effort for "truth, justice, and the American way."

The lunch box reflected a daily image of a character, a setting, and a role model for children during a unique era. The few heroes described herein are perhaps the most famous in a broad list of names and roles. Each made lasting impressions on the lives of millions. Oh, those lunchbox heroes! Let's bring them back for an encore!

## Reasoning

1. The primary focus of the selection is to   (*a*) relate the entertainment value of early television programs   (*b*) look at how television has developed better profits from commercials   (*c*) promote the use of television to teach values to children   (*d*) develop new programs of instructional value for children.

2. How did the author probably gather the research with which to write the selection?   (*a*) informal interviews and personal experiences   (*b*) informal interviews and television ratings   (*c*) formal research and history study   (*d*) psychology and sociology findings and formal interviews with professionals.

3. According to this article, the period of 1800–1900 in American history was one of   (*a*) rapid change and equal rights   (*b*) slow change and few values   (*c*) law and order and the cowboy as a central figure   (*d*) Indian rights and law and order.

4. Television probably represented the frontier characters in the selection in which of the following manners?   (*a*) historically accurate   (*b*) with fewer values than in real life   (*c*) with more values than in real life   (*d*) with less appeal to adult audiences

5. The focus of change in television throughout the 1950's mostly related to
(*a*) improved technology  (*b*) increased commercials  (*c*) school use  (*d*) different programs.

_____

## Theme

6. An appropriate pair of theme words for the selection might be  (*a*) entertainment
and profits  (*b*) nostalgia and historical accounts  (*c*) progress and role models
(*d*) nostalgia and role models.

_____

7. Choose one character from the selection and match an appropriate theme word
from the selection with that character. Choose another well-known character from
television or movies today who also fits that theme word. (For example: Teenage
Ninja Turtles represent forces of good against forces of evil.)

_____

_____

_____

## Author's Purpose or Bias

8. The author's main purpose in writing this selection is to  (*a*) inform parents to
monitor the programs that children watch  (*b*) request business to bring back
programs from the 50's  (*c*) establish a balance of programs to teach history to
children through television  (*d*) remind people that values can be taught through
television.

_____

9. The author's biases are brought to the reader through  (*a*) praise  (*b*) sarcasm
(*c*) humor  (*d*) seriousness.

_____

10. The author probably has a bias toward  (*a*) current advertising techniques on
television  (*b*) current school subjects  (*c*) effect of television on children
(*d*) television sponsors not supporting programs from the 50's.

_____

## Applying the Skills in Content Subjects

### LANGUAGE ARTS PRACTICE A

**PREREADING**   The piggy bank and the rainy day, two symbols of saving money.
Are you a "saver" or a "spender"? How important is the category?

I recently stood in a department store check-out line, patiently awaiting the opportunity to part with two dollars and change for flashlight batteries. My eye caught the neatly packaged and colorful display of disposable flashlights for an equal amount. Sentimental value prevailed. Before me stood a finger-tapping, sneaker-shuffling, gum-chomping lad of fifteen or so eagerly extending four crisp twenties for two video games. His sneakers had some orange pump gadget to improve jumping ability. I guessed that they came in handy as he improved the video scores and wanted to jump for joy. Otherwise, a basketball would have been neatly tucked under the left arm. Memories of a semester's tuition or an "as-is" used car flashed back as purchasing power proximities to the tab for two video games and a pair of sneakers. Just the sneaker price tag exceeded the cost to adorn my toes and heels throughout high school.

A quick stop at the dry cleaners for two business suits brought the tribulation of witnessing a seventeen-year-old miss picking up an arrangement of sweaters, jeans, a parka, three pairs of slacks, and a prom dress. The total—$62.75 or, better still, an amount equal to an entire spring wardrobe for my sister in her teenage heyday.

One last shopping stop at the auto parts store for five quarts of oil and one filter for my rusty, but trusty, eighty-two-thousand-mile four-door brought the spending and savings habits of younger Americans into alarming focus. As I opened the door, a sleek, black, pin-striped, alloy-wheeled, moon-roofed two-door, equal in worth to my first home, screeched to a polite halt in the adjoining space. A sun-glassed, gold-chained, perfectly coiffed young gent of eighteen or so angled out and sauntered across the parking lot. Paying for my eight-dollar purchase, I could not resist the temptation of beholding the total for the young gent behind me. A double zip of the jacket, one check of the bag, and a deliberate wallet audit ended with the announcement. One-hundred and eighty-two dollars for two stereo speakers to replace the inferior manufacturer's brand. I almost cried!

What has become of the value of money and saving money among the younger generations? What happened to that rainy-day proverb that existed some years back? I've read the studies that show more younger Americans working than ever before. Those same studies proclaim the 12–20 age group as having the most expendable income.

And spend they do! But hasn't this proclivity for spending brought a diminished priority for saving?

How about a little for the bank account or maybe a savings bond or two each month? Join the credit union of a parent or invest in a low risk mutual fund. Learn about the stock market at home or at school and risk a few dollars for investment with family or friends. How about some form of financial planning agenda?

Okay, okay, those days are gone. Live for today. Look good and feel good. You can't take it with you and you earned it, so you've got the right to spend it. You'll be an adult for a long time. Have fun, fun, fun, till somebody or something takes the T'bird and leisure spending power away!

I guess "a penny saved is a penny earned" has evolved into "a penny earned is a penny burned"! I knew that money burned holes in some pockets, but never that teenagers carried little blowtorches! Next time, I'm shopping with earplugs and blinders.

Oh no, there I go again—trying to impose old-fashioned habits on newer generations! Go for it, soar with the eagles, be happy! Wait a minute . . . .

## *Reasoning*

1. The word "coiffed" as used in the selection refers to   (*a*) behavior   (*b*) appearance   (*c*) manners   (*d*) physical condition.

_____

2. The three experiences in the selection are intended to   (*a*) amuse and teach   (*b*) give examples and warnings   (*c*) discourage spending and wasting   (*d*) relate examples and habits.

_____

3. The comment "I almost cried" indicates the author's reaction to   (*a*) the price of the speakers   (*b*) the reason for the purchase   (*c*) the comparison of his car to the young man's car   (*d*) what that amount of money would purchase in the author's youth. Explain your answer in one sentence.

_____

_____

4. The author's discussions about savings habits are most like which of the following? (*a*) whether to do homework or go out with friends   (*b*) whether to read a book or play tennis   (*c*) whether to go on a cruise vacation or buy a needed second car   (*d*) whether to call long distance or write a letter

_____

5. Which side of the "save" or "spend" argument, as presented by the author, do you support and follow? Give two of the author's reasons and two of your own to support your position.

_____

_____

_____

6. The author's philosophy about the younger generation is   (*a*) they should develop lifelong spending habits   (*b*) they do not understand the value of work   (*c*) they should be more concerned with school than work   (*d*) they should take more risks with investments.

_____

## *Theme*

7. What theme is displayed by the young man at the auto parts store? Explain your answer.

_____

_____

8. Which of the following words or phrases from the selection is the best theme for the entire selection? (*a*) tribulation (*b*) temptation (*c*) purchasing power (*d*) habitual saving. Explain your answer in one sentence.

_____

## *Author's Purpose or Bias*

9. The author's purpose to discuss spending and saving habits is brought out through a tone of (*a*) humor and indifference (*b*) sarcasm and concern (*c*) seriousness and advice (*d*) humor and warning.

_____

10. The author shows a bias against people who (*a*) don't spend money (*b*) don't work for spending money (*c*) don't invest money (*d*) don't avoid wasting money.

_____

## LANGUAGE ARTS PRACTICE B

**PREREADING** The traditional role of the teacher is to impart knowledge, and the role of the student is to learn from that knowledge. What happens to the learning experience when the roles are reversed?

"Winter Oak" is a beautifully penned short story by Yuri Nagibin, a Russian writer relatively unknown in America. Two modest and un-assuming main characters are set in a small Russian village as Nagibin narrates the circumstances of a January school day. The simple but unique events, experiences, and feelings of a twenty-four-year-old schoolteacher, Anna Vasilyevna, and a ten-year-old student, Savushkin, are played out in charming language—language that pleases the mind, warms the heart, and satisfies the soul. A rare translation of "Winter Oak" appears in the September, 1979, issue of the *Atlantic Monthly*.

Admired and respected by parents and citizens of the village and countryside, Anna is teaching a lesson on nouns to her class. The children are always obedient and attentive to her strict manner and structured lessons. Savushkin arrives tardy, as usual, and slides into his seat with snow covering his tattered clothes and oversized battered boots, but sporting a healthy look with red-rosey cheeks and a smile from ear to ear. A few minutes later, when queried to give an example of a noun during the language lesson, Savushkin offers "winter oak." Anna informs him that "oak" is the noun and "winter" as used is a word to be studied later. Savushkin receives a prod with the warning that he is in trouble now.

At recess Anna sits Savushkin down to lecture him about constant tardiness, indifference to the rules of the class, and lack of study. With patience stretched to the limit, she will walk him home that afternoon and speak with his mother to solve these annoyances once and for all.

The two set out to trek the half-hour journey that always occupied forty-five minutes to one hour of Savushkin's time twice each school day. The winter path winds along the frozen brook where birch trees extend bare fingers into the deep blue and sunshine-painted sky. Elk, rabbit, and other animal tracks of all sizes are pressed into glistening snow. Savushkin explains the sources of each and the variety of droppings, while Anna asks about the openings in the brook. Savushkin points to a small, warm, bubbling spring just barely visible to the naked eye. A small pond receives the brook's slight flow as Savushkin aims the discussion to the thick ice with a variety of protruding plants, each absorbing the radiant sunshine.

Suddenly, in an opening ahead, a magnificent oak tree stands like a monument before them. Savushkin takes Anna by the hand to its broad trunk and gently brushes away the snow and dead leaves. Like a penny-candy shopping spree, Savushkin remarks and relates the pristine world of the winter oak and nature's cold-weather display of innocent occupants. Anna beams with fascination at the bugs, spiders, lizards, and even a hibernating hedgehog as the little boy spins observations into a quilt of commentary.

Anna looks at her watch as Savushkin informs her that his mother has probably left for work and that no one would be home to speak with her. Abruptly, Anna Vasilyevna informs Savushkin to follow the highway to school and not to take the shortcut path through the forest again. She thanks him for the scenic walk and informative tour, and with a youthful wink, states: "I didn't mean what I just told you. Of course you can take the forest path to school."

As Anna turns to follow the same return path to the village, Savushkin breaks off a thin tree limb and passes it to Anna. Smiling from ear to ear, his advice is to confront any elk in her path with a light tap on its back. Or better still, to wave the stick and give a mild holler so it won't leave the forest for good.

## Reasoning

1. The author of this selection is most impressed with Yuri Nagibin's (*a*) insight and understanding of people (*b*) background understanding of teaching and learning (*c*) use of language to convey a story (*d*) insight and understanding of Russia.

2. The original and the translation of "Winter Oak" are primarily what type of writing? (*a*) instructional with examples (*b*) narration and description (*c*) opinions with supporting facts (*d*) persuasive with one argument

_____

3. The parents and citizens of the village admired and respected Anna because she (*a*) allowed her students to develop at their own ability levels (*b*) had rules to follow for strict discipline (*c*) encouraged children to participate in class (*d*) maintained constant communication with the home.

_____

4. The two contrasting teaching and learning processes exhibited by Anna and Savushkin relate respectively to (*a*) discipline and punishment (*b*) classroom instruction and homework (*c*) books and observation (*d*) school rules and parent support. Explain which one you favor with at least one good reason.

_____

_____

_____

5. Why does Anna first tell Savushkin that he cannot take the shortcut, and then quickly change her mind? (*a*) she wants to remain his friend (*b*) she does not want him to lose his enthusiasm (*c*) she will trade the right for being on time (*d*) she will ask him to bring examples of nature to class

_____

6. Explain two thoughts that may have preoccupied Anna's thinking during her return walk to the village.

_____

_____

_____

_____

## Theme

7. An appropriate pair of theme words for the relationship between Anna and Savushkin are (*a*) dissension and reconciliation (*b*) sharing and understanding (*c*) envy and cooperation (*d*) immaturity and maturation.

_____

8. Compare the theme of this selection to that of a story or television program or movie. Explain the comparison by using a theme word or phrase of your own.

_____

_____

_____

_____

## *Author's Purpose or Bias*

9. The author's purpose in relating Nagibin's short story is to (*a*) show how difficult it is to discipline children (*b*) describe why teachers must relate to parents (*c*) give an example of the teacher-student learning process (*d*) support the need for using field trips to expose children to the world.

---

10. It would seem that both Yuri Nagibin and the author of the selection are biased against teachers who (*a*) use only books to teach (*b*) allow students to disregard rules (*c*) do not communicate with parents (*d*) show displeasure toward a student in front of the class.

---

## LANGUAGE ARTS PRACTICE C

**PREREADING**   America has been the industrial and economic world leader for many decades. What is the forecast into the 21st century for maintaining this stature? Or the reasons for losing such a standing?

Millie runs a little store in Coon Rapids, Minn., a suburb of Minneapolis. It's a "mom and pop" operation that competes with the 7-Eleven type chains. If press reports and economic projections are right, independent stores like Millie's may soon be as extinct as the dodo bird. Millie's, though, has prospered.

It thrives because Millie is behind the counter every day from 8:30 in the morning until nine at night. She is there Christmas Eve, New Year's Eve, the Fourth of July, Thanksgiving, her own birthday. She was even there the day after her husband's funeral.

Her store isn't much bigger than the average bedroom, yet in that small space she has somehow managed to cram every conceivable type of supply anyone could need. When my wife wanted a strange spice whose name I've since forgotten, Millie had it. When I needed a 6¼ amp fuse—something that's hard to find in many hardware stores—Millie had it.

People come to Millie's for more than just soda pop, snack foods, cereal, hot dogs, or hamburgers. They come for the conversation about everything from the baseball standings to who just had a baby. They come because Millie doesn't ask for your ID when you cash a check or food stamps, and if you happen to be a dollar short, Millie will tell you it's okay to pay later. They come because Millie has helped out a fair number of families who happened to be down on their luck. And they come because, like my four-year-old, they were allowed to choose free pieces of candy as toddlers and have been coming back ever since.

Millie's way of doing business is close to a lost art. To her, the old slogan "The customer is always right" still means something. Everyone who walks in the door is treated with the same courtesy and respect— from those who drive Mercedes to men in flannel work shirts who drive old pickups. At Millie's there are no invisible customers.

Anyone who has flown on a domestic airliner, had a car repaired, eaten at a restaurant or shopped in a department store knows what it's like to be an invisible customer. And a lot of those invisible customers end up with shoddy products. Many of us are rebelling, flooding Better Business Bureaus with complaints, and deserting U.S. products for foreign competitors. America has been losing its world market share because we have lost sight of what we once knew how to do almost by instinct.

Americans have not always been the first to invent something or to have the most advanced technology. But in the past we have always been able to take an idea, expand upon it, and give the customer value and service. The gasoline-powered car was developed by the Germans, but it was an American who gave the customer a cheap, reliable vehicle with a simple design. "Any color, so long as it's black," said Henry Ford. The Germans were also the first to use jet airplanes, but it was the Americans who eventually capitalized on the commercial possibilities of jet aviation.

Quality is not a complex matter. It boils down to serving customers in such a way that they keep coming back. Nor are business ethics all that complex. Customer service is a concept rooted in the rule "Serve others as you yourself would wish to be served." Business scandals show that a lot of people serve only themselves. Millie could have told them that, but then the management gurus and business press aren't interviewing people like Millie. Perhaps they need to get out of their plush suites and visit the heartlands, where they will find places like Millie's. They would learn some valuable survival lessons.

## Reasoning

*1.* Give three reasons why Millie was at the store the day after her husband's funeral.

_____

_____

_____

*2.* All of the following would be customary of Millie EXCEPT  (*a*) the purchase of Girl Scout cookies from a neighborhood child  (*b*) attendance at the church bazaar  (*c*) interest in a dignitary's visit  (*d*) food donation for a family burned out of their home.

_____

Explain your answer in one sentence.

_____

*3.* What quality of Millie's character does the author seem to most respect?  (*a*) her support for local charities  (*b*) her support for selling American products  (*c*) her treatment of and attitude toward customers  (*d*) her ideas offered to other businesses

_____

4. The primary focus of the selection is on  (*a*) the takeover of family businesses in America  (*b*) the relationship of customer service to business in America  (*c*) the product quality of other countries compared to that of America  (*d*) the decline of American ingenuity in product development.

_____

5. Give three specific contrasts between Millie's store and a 7-Eleven or fast-food place in your neighborhood.

_____

_____

_____

6. Give three examples of the loss that Coon Rapids, Minnesota, will experience when Millie retires or the store closes.

_____

_____

_____

## Theme

7. The theme of quality relates best to Millie in which one of the following?
(*a*) the products she sold  (*b*) the service she offered  (*c*) her dedication to community  (*d*) her personality

_____

8. The theme of survival as related in the last sentence refers to  (*a*) people being able to earn a decent salary  (*b*) business being able to compete with foreign countries  (*c*) American products being better built than foreign competitors  (*d*) American business practicing better ethics.

_____

## Author's Purpose or Bias

9. The author wrote this selection to  (*a*) relate an experience for developing small businesses  (*b*) show values that are absent in American business practices  (*c*) relate the simplicity of good business practices  (*d*) issue a warning for business to follow foreign practices.

_____

10. The author is biased in favor of  (*a*) honesty and hard work  (*b*) women demonstrating independence  (*c*) government prosecuting Wall Street scandals  (*d*) families starting their own businesses

_____

# SOCIAL STUDIES PRACTICE A

**PREREADING**  Who were the greatest athletes of all time? Which athletic performances rank among the greatest? What were the reasons for such great performances?

Ted Williams in the 40's, Rocky Marciano in the 50's, Jim Brown in the 60's, Chris Evert in the 70's, Larry Bird in the 80's, and Michael Jordan in the 90's—all symbolizing brilliant rays of light in the laser show of athletic accomplishment in American sports history. Volumes of other names complement this cluster of sports notables with name and event and date and statistic and honor chronicling the lofty level of achievement for each. Ability is often at the apex of performance. But what are the forces that support the underlying motivation to compete, to bring passion with performance, to confront and overcome adversity? Is there a creed or oath which brings sports beyond the rules of the game? What constitutes a truly great athletic performance and accomplishment?

"The most important thing is not to win, but to take part, just as the most important thing in life is not the triumph but the struggle. The essential thing is not to have conquered but to have fought well." This is the creed of the Olympic Games.

"In the name of all competitors I promise that we will take part, respecting and abiding by the rules which govern, in the true spirit of sportsmanship for the glory of sport and the honor of our teams." This is the oath taken by each participating athlete in the Olympic Games.

Americans have enshrined many professional and Olympic athletes in the showcases of performance and accomplishment. What were the extenuating circumstances, if any, for the most memorable? How much did fan support contribute to the victory? Perhaps the decade previous to Ted Williams and the historical setting of Berlin, Germany, provided the time and place and circumstance for the greatest athletic performance in American sports history.

This was the era in world history just prior to World War II—a time of superheated emotional motivation, perhaps inspired by the Olympic creed and oath. But certainly a time of German racial motivation. It was this unique clash of time and attitude that set the stage, and perhaps, the reasons for athletic greatness.

Adolf Hitler was dictator of Germany as the Third Reich was evolving into a power that would change history through today. Hosted in Berlin, the 1936 Olympic Games were to be Hitler's arena for not only sports, but more important his display of "Aryans," a term referring to certain races of Europeans. The Aryans were primarily Germans in Hitler's eyes and, thus, people superior to other races. This attitude would eventually serve Hitler's maniacal desire for genocide, the holocaust, the obsession for victory in World War II.

One brief moment in history brought Adolf Hitler and a young black American son of a sharecropper together in the same arena. Hitler and thousands of Germans would prove Aryan supremacy with German athletes trouncing all competition. Jesse Owens embarrassed Hitler and Germany by winning four gold medals in track and field events, both individual and team. He went on to set seven world records during his athletic career and to serve the community and young people. Owens gave many speeches supporting clean living, fair play, and patriotism right up to his death in 1980. One can only speculate on the atmosphere of the stadium in Berlin in 1936 as the announcement echoed around the world to "Let the Games Begin." And the contributions that Jesse Owens brought to history.

## Reasoning

1. The primary focus of the selection relates to  (*a*) the effect of adversity on increasing athletic performance  (*b*) whether adversity affects athletic performance  (*c*) the impact of the site of the Olympic Games on athletic performance  (*d*) how one athlete can affect the image of the Olympic Games.

_____

2. Which of the following was Adolf Hitler most concerned with in 1936?  (*a*) establishing the Aryan image in the world  (*b*) winning the most gold medals in the 1936 Olympic Games  (*c*) defeating American athletes whom he viewed as a threat to German supremacy  (*d*) avoiding a loss of momentum in developing the Third Reich

_____

Explain your answer with one specific reason.

_____

_____

3. Given the time in history, how could the circumstances of the Olympic Games and Hitler's attitude concerning Aryans have been avoided?  (*a*) black athletes could have boycotted the Games  (*b*) America could have boycotted the Games  (*c*) the host city of Berlin could have been changed  (*d*) the creed and oath of the games could have been rewritten

_____

Explain why you think such a decision was not made.

_____

_____

4. List three factors mentioned in the selection that contributed to great athletic performance in 1936.

   Hitler proving aryahn supremesy, the holocaust, WWII

List three factors not mentioned in this selection that you believe also contribute to great athletic performance today.

_medical enhansment, good coachings and representing your country_

5. The attitude of the author toward the athletes named in the selection is one of (**a**) great respect (**b**) great pride (**c**) great support (**d**) great memories

6. Which do you feel is more important to the image of the Olympic Games and sports in general—the Olympic creed or the oath? Give two reasons for your answer.

_the oath is more important than winning and proved good sportsmanship._

## Theme

7. The best pair of theme words relating to Hitler as presented in the selection are (**a**) greed and power (**b**) politics and obsession (**c**) conflict and prejudice (**d**) prejudice and domination.

8. The best pair of theme words relating to the life of Jesse Owens as presented in the selection are (**a**) motivation and patriotism (**b**) individualism and education (**c**) indolence and perseverance (**d**) tyranny and freedom.

## Author's Purpose or Bias

9. The author's purpose in writing this selection is to (**a**) reflect upon the memorable accomplishments of American athletes (**b**) describe the problems that can affect athletic performance (**c**) show how the Olympic Games have changed (**d**) relate an event for recollection and consideration.

10. The author is biased against athletic competition that does not reflect (**a**) fair play by the athletes (**b**) hospitality by the home team (**c**) written rules to abide by (**d**) winning athletes giving some service to the community.

## SOCIAL STUDIES PRACTICE B

**PREREADING**   Would more school days during the year mean more learning for American students? Take some time to consider your answer and the reasons for that answer.

The founding Fathers guaranteed it in the Constitution written in the 1700's. Horace Mann was the inspirational and organizational figure who established its beginnings and growth in the 1800's. Throughout most of the 1900's, it always enjoyed the status of delivering the American dream. But as the centuries merge twenty into twenty-one, the issue of public education and its services and role in preparing young people to take their places in society has come under intense study. Recommendations for change are boiling in the kettle and the whistle is about to scream for action.

The school calendar of six hours a day and 180 days a year has its roots in colonial life-style. Children often trudged long distances to school and back. After-school responsibilities on the farm and in the home were assumed seven days a week. Spring was the season of planting, summer the season of growing, fall the season of harvesting, and winter the season of surviving and preparing for spring. Education was a priority of the family, but work ranked higher.

Throughout most of the 20th century, the industrial society brought a reduction in farms and physical labor. Demands on public schools to foster expanded skills and services began to increase. These expectations included not only the 3 R's, but also preparation for college and participation in extra-curricular activities and athletics—all within a status-quo school day and yearly calendar. Enter two compelling arguments for expanding the school year from 180 days to 220 or more days.

Argument #1: The American family now consists predominantly of one single working parent or two parents working full time. Too many children now confront empty hours with little supervision after school. This time would be better spent expanding the learning experience. More school days would reduce time necessary to review or reteach the work of the previous year. Enrichment programs would provide learning and social experiences denied by the current calendar. Student performance on tests would improve. Less television exposure would result. A longer school year would buoy parent and citizen support for community schools.

Argument #2: America has remained a tenuously leading player in a global economy and changing world order of countries. Most of these countries spend more money on public education and require a longer school day and/or year than the United States. Japan, Germany, and Thailand are just a few in a list striving to develop a better educated citizen. A longer school year would discipline young Americans to the rigors of a forty-plus hour workweek. Most children in competing countries study English as a second language in elementary school. Fluency is the objective. A longer school year would also provide better opportunities for mastery of English among the growing immigrant population in America.

Additional reasons for either argument exist. Additional arguments have been and will continue to be offered in defense of a longer school year. "When" and "how" are immediate questions for proactive (anticipating future problems) planning. A reactive answer to the future question "Why wasn't the school year ever expanded?" may reflect a society in unfortunate decline.

## Reasoning

*1.* The reason for guaranteeing and providing public education in the 1700's and 1800's best related to the need to  (*a*) prepare children for the world of work  (*b*) develop better methods of farming  (*c*) give children some sense of history  (*d*) uphold the requirements of the Constitution.

_____

*2.* According to the selection, demands on public schools to expand services throughout the 1900's were caused primarily because  (*a*) the economic and social base of American society changed  (*b*) children needed different ways to occupy more free time  (*c*) business established literacy requirements for employment  (*d*) parents opted for private schools.

_____

*3.* The primary difference between the two arguments for a longer school year relates to reasons of  (*a*) cost and return  (*b*) students and increased accomplishments  (*c*) utilization of schools and personnel  (*d*) education and preparation.

_____

*4.* Which of the two arguments do you most support? Give the two most important reasons from the selection and two reasons of your own related to the premise of the argument.

_____

_____

_____


*5.* It would seem that the most crucial concern for a longer school year would be addressing the need for  (*a*) retraining teachers for a longer school year  (*b*) financing a longer school year  (*c*) modifying school buildings for a longer school year  (*d*) avoiding disruptions in the family with a longer school year.

_____

*6.* The tone of the last paragraph is one of  (*a*) admonition  (*b*) condemnation  (*c*) frustration  (*d*) consternation.

_____

## Theme

7. The concept of the "American dream" best relates to the theme of   (*a*) status
(*b*) preparation   (*c*) opportunity   (*d*) change.

_____

Explain your answer.

_____

_____

8. The fact that the 180-day school year has not changed for the most part since the 1700's would relate best to what theme in public education?   (*a*) innovation
(*b*) progress   (*c*) deprivation   (*d*) stagnation

_____

## Author's Purpose or Bias

9. The purpose of the selection is to encourage   (*a*) planning and change   (*b*) input and support   (*c*) status quo and funding   (*d*) parental support and action

_____

10. The author most sides with   (*a*) removing the Constitutional provision for public education   (*b*) improving the quality of services in public schools   (*c*) modeling our schools on the education services of foreign countries   (*d*) funding more after school programs.

_____

### SOCIAL STUDIES PRACTICE C

**PREREADING**   Many voters and taxpayers are concerned about the government and the decision-making process. Are too many decisions made in favor of business and campaign supporters instead of the average citizen? If so, what action can be taken to force elected officials to be more responsible to the average citizen?

Every year millions of taxpayers get their federal tax-return forms. Four out of five of them will check the "no" box on the line that asks whether $1 of their tax payment can go to the presidential campaign fund.

That's unfortunate at best. Marking the "yes" box won't decrease your refund. It won't increase your tax bill. It will shrink by $1 what otherwise would go to other federal programs—and buy the cheapest insurance available against getting stuck with a president beholden only to special-interest groups.

Such interest groups offer one thing candidates must have: money, lots of it. Just making a serious primary bid will cost at least $6 million. Nabbing a nomination will take $21 million more. Presidential hopefuls will have spent $375 million by November's election.

Small wonder special-interest cash can offer such an alluring mud bath. Small wonder public financing has proven one of the few brushes able to scrub off the dirt that can take over campaigns. Congress created the presidential campaign fund in the 1970's to try to end such abuses. Here's how it works:

1. Both taxpayer and candidate participation must be voluntary.
2. Primary candidates can get federal funds to match donations of $250 or less from individuals only—not from special interests or political parties.
3. Major party nominees get a preset amount—$46 million each in 1988—but must limit spending and refuse any money from individuals or special interests.

When the White House is the goal, no system offers ironclad guarantees against chicanery, but public financing has gone far to remove temptation. Still, only 19.9% of taxpayers gave to the fund last year, down from 28.7% a decade ago. Sen. Mitch McConnell, R-KY, theorizes that many just don't want their money spent on politics.

That's understandable, but if this public financing plan falls short anywhere, it's that it doesn't extend to Congress. After all, $1 is a small price to pay to free our highest elected officials from the chains of special-interest money.

## *Reasoning*

1. Taxpayers who check "no" on their tax return are most likely to be expressing a dissatisfaction with   (*a*) the slate of candidates   (*b*) most federal programs   (*c*) spending money on politics   (*d*) income-tax laws.

2. The selection is concerned with   (*a*) allowing a taxpayer to voluntarily increase a donation to the election fund   (*b*) mandating the $1 donation to the election fund   (*c*) discontinuing the presidential election fund   (*d*) extending the purpose and rules of the fund to Congress.

3. Which of the following circumstances DO NOT relate to the word "chicanery" as used in the selection?   (*a*) plagiarism to improve grades   (*b*) lowering prices to attract customers and defeat competition   (*c*) television advertising to increase profits   (*d*) embezzling funds as a bank employee

4. More taxpayers might contribute $1 to the fund if   (*a*) more candidates sought public office   (*b*) the money did not reduce other federal programs   (*c*) federal matching funds were increased   (*d*) the $250 maximum contribution were reduced.

5. One of the author's major concerns is that   (*a*) presidential campaigns have become too expensive   (*b*) presidential candidates have not earned the public

trust   (*c*) special-interest groups have too much influence   (*d*) special-interest groups should have more influence.

6. Argue for or against Sen. McConnell's theory. Give two reasons from the selection and one reason of your own to support your position.

_____

_____

_____

## *Theme*

7. Choose what you think is the best theme word in the selection and explain your choice.

_____

_____

_____

8. The best pair of theme words for the selection might be   (*a*) power and greed   (*b*) legislation and control   (*c*) charity and accountability   (*d*) deception and patronage.

_____

## *Author's Purpose or Bias*

9. The author's purpose is to persuade the reader through which one of the following?   (*a*) relating examples and statistics   (*b*) narrating and describing historical situations   (*c*) facts and opinions   (*d*) emotional pleas

_____

10. Which one of the following would best summarize the author's view or bias? (*a*) Check "no" and increase funding for non-political federal programs   (*b*) Enact laws to reduce escalating and costly presidential campaigns   (*c*) Help keep presidential candidates free of obligations to special-interest groups   (*d*) Establish laws denying special-interest groups the opportunity to contribute to presidential candidates

_____

## SCIENCE PRACTICE A

**PREREADING**   Rarely do man and nature meet in the most extreme conditions for both survival and conquest. Consider one of the most memorable events.

In March 1990, an international team of six adventurers and 36 sled dogs completed a trek without precedent in the history of exploration: They crossed the breadth of Antarctica on foot. But Minnesotan Will

Steger, who in 1986 led the first self-contained dogsled expedition to the North Pole, barely survived at the bottom of the world. "I must admit I have experienced some near-hopeless moments here," he wrote in his journal.

Battling constant storms and exhaustion, men and animals braved the harshest wilderness on Earth for 220 grueling days in 1990. They covered, remarkably, 3,741 miles by sled and ski, quaking in temperatures of 60 below zero (wind chills of 150 below), inching across rolling waves of ice riddled with deadly hidden crevasses, traversing mountain ranges as high as 11,400 feet.

A throwback to the great polar feats of the turn of the century, the Trans-Antarctica Expedition was filled with infectious enthusiasm and an anything's possible 1960's feel. Network TV covered it. Thousands of volunteers lent a hand. About 15 million schoolchildren worldwide monitored the progress and learned why the seventh continent must be preserved from exploitation. Although the US government icily viewed the adventure as a stunt, the Soviets, Chinese, and Japanese rallied with manpower and support.

Along with cold, wind, and whiteouts, daily irritants included frostbite, snowblindness, sunburn, altitude sickness, and hypothermia. "Moisture is our mortal enemy," Steger noted; "drying is our savior."

In September, wind-whipped snow coated the inside of the explorers' mouths when they gulped for breath, nearly suffocating them. In October, Steger wrote, "the wind chills were at the limit of what a warm-blooded creature could stand. Any exposed skin on our faces froze." Fifty-three days out, after being laid low by weather, Steger pulled out his National Geographic map of Antarctica and realized that in nearly two months, he had traveled only about four inches. "We still have two feet to go," he wrote.

In December, the team attained the South Pole. In January and February, they became the first humans to cross the aptly named Area of Inaccessibility, and in March they slogged on to the opposite side of the continent. But Steger constantly was reminded of the earlier British explorer, Robert Falcon Scott, and his dying charge that Antarctica is an "awful place; the expedition took on periods of farce, tantrums, and mortal peril."

Steger believes in the nobility of the human spirit and the near-mystical wonder of dog power. He's no literary stylist, but Jon Bowermaster is, and he boils Steger's journal into a crisply moving, clean book. *Crossing Antarctica* is a winsome tale destined to join the classics of exploration.

**Peter Gorner**

## Reasoning

*1.* Give two reasons of your own for "why the seventh continent must be preserved from exploitation."

2. What was the greatest motivation to accomplish the seven-month journey?
   (*a*) having worldwide support   (*b*) getting the notoriety upon conclusion
   (*c*) being the first to cross Antarctica on foot   (*d*) keeping daily records
   for history

   _____

3. Steger probably believes that the journey was successful because of the   (*a*) television coverage   (*b*) dogs   (*c*) volunteers   (*d*) National Geographic maps.

   _____

4. What two qualities were most needed by the individual explorers to accomplish
   the journey?   (*a*) physical stamina and compatibility   (*b*) physical stamina and
   understanding of geography   (*c*) physical stamina and medical knowledge
   (*d*) physical stamina and mental stamina
   Explain your answer.

   _____

   _____

   _____

5. Explain the statement by the earlier explorer, Robert Falcon Scott: "the expedition
   took on periods of farce, tantrums, and mortal peril."

   _____

   _____

   _____

6. The subtle focus of the selection is to   (*a*) give a firsthand account of a great
   adventure   (*b*) encourage you to read *Crossing Antarctica*   (*c*) show that Will
   Steger is an American to be proud of   (*d*) develop support against the exploitation
   of Antarctica.

   _____

## Theme

7. The best theme word(s) from the selection about the expedition would be
   (*a*) exhaustion   (*b*) progress   (*c*) survival   (*d*) mortal peril.

   _____

8. The theme of "the nobility of the human spirit" as it relates to the explorers best
   compares to the themes of   (*a*) friendship and sacrifice   (*b*) traversing and suffocating   (*c*) experience and exploration   (*d*) stamina and determination.

   _____

   Copy three phrases from the selection that reflect these themes.

   _____

   _____

   _____

## *Author's Purpose or Bias*

9. The author's purpose for writing this selection is to   (*a*) inform   (*b*) persuade   (*c*) ask questions   (*d*) give answers.

_____

10. The author is biased in support of people who are   (*a*) educated   (*b*) gregarious   (*c*) independent   (*d*) aggressive
Explain your answer.

_____

_____

### SCIENCE PRACTICE B

**PREREADING**   The world is running out of fresh-water supplies. What should you know to help slow the flow of this problem? What can you do about it?

"Water, water everywhere, but not a drop to drink" is a saying that might describe survival at sea while drifting aimlessly in a life raft. But consider the application of the adage to American life-style into the 21st century. Consider the water resources of the planet, the forces of nature and man, and the consumption demands of industry and people. Consider the immediate need for each and every man, woman, and child to recognize, understand, and act upon the "water forecast" of dwindling supplies followed by spiraling costs and austere changes in American life-style.

Comprised of 25% land and 75% water, Earth has the physical appearance of an unlimited supply of water. However, only 3% is fresh water and 2% of that 3% (or 65–70% of all fresh water) is frozen at the polar caps. Thus, 1% or 1 of every 100 gallons of water is available for human use. And that 1% is constantly subjected to the forces of nature and man.

Clearly, the most serious forces of nature and man on fresh-water reserves are drought and pollution, respectively. Drought is a major problem because most water supplies are underground, stored in nature's aquifers. When drought persists, withdrawal of water from the aquifers increases since surface water is reduced or depleted. Aquifers are replenished through absorption of surface water into the ground. When rain finally arrives, much of it often runs off the dry ground into rivers or evaporates back into the atmosphere. Thus, the absorption process is inhibited and aquifers are not fully replenished.

Pollution is the result of discharging toxic chemicals directly into the air or surface water. Pollutants discharged into the air are often returned to earth in rain or snow. Any pollution increases the likelihood of absorption into the aquifers. The polluting partners in America are many, but industry and automobiles lead the pack.

Now add these results of drought and pollution to increasing consumption demands of industry and people. Taxing water supplies at an average daily rate of 70 gallons or 25,000–30,000 gallons a year by each American may be a sobering statistic. But not in comparison to the fact that agricultural industries swallow 80% of all the fresh water consumed annually. Both industry and individuals will have to pay the piper for years of rock-bottom prices and indiscriminate use and waste of fresh water.

Evaporation of surface water during farming irrigation is wasted water. The average home is a mirror of water-wasting activity from flushing the toilet to washing the clothes, dishes, and car. Ironically, the actual drinking of water ranks at the bottom of the consumption list and at the top of the efficient use list. How will necessary supplies be maintained? When and at what price will escalating costs peak?

Recommendations to float icebergs from the northern polar caps or construct massive desalination plants are answers offered to the question of supply. Hundreds and, eventually, thousands of dollars a year into the 21st century are projected for the average family, answering the question of water cost. Gulp! How do we begin to protect and plan the consumption of fresh water or face serious problems for farmers, inconveniences to life-style, and costs that drain the pocketbook?

## *Reasoning*

1. In the first paragraph and throughout most of the selection, the author wants the reader to  (*a*) act  (*b*) discuss  (*c*) think  (*d*) research.

_____

2. All of the following would bring "inconvenient changes in American life-style" EXCEPT  (*a*) bans on washing cars and lawns  (*b*) using polluted aquifers for irrigation  (*c*) fines for excess water consumption  (*d*) government regulation of desalination plants.

_____

3. Which of the following has the most impact on maintaining adequate and usable water supplies?  (*a*) consistent drought-free weather  (*b*) pollution-free aquifers  (*c*) government regulations capping industry and home consumption  (*d*) industry developing new sources of water supply

_____

4. Which of the following could serve as the best example of "pay the piper" resulting from lack of attention to water problems?  (*a*) less water—increased car wash prices  (*b*) polluted water—increased drinking water prices  (*c*) polluted water—increased food prices  (*d*) less water—loss of agricultural jobs
Explain your answer.

_____

_____

_____

5. The selection provides enough information to answer each of the following questions EXCEPT (*a*) What is the ratio of land mass to water mass on earth? (*b*) How are aquifers affected by the agricultural and automobile industries? (*c*) What are the possible alternatives to increasing water supplies? (*d*) What effects will reduced or polluted water supplies have on the future health of Americans?

_____

6. Name three things or programs that you could use or follow at home to conserve water.

_____

_____

_____

## *Theme*

7. The dominating theme word from the selection is (*a*) water pollution (*b*) water consumption (*c*) water desalination (*d*) water evaporation.
   Explain your answer.

_____

_____

_____

8. Choose a theme word or phrase of your own and explain how it applies to the selection.

_____

_____

_____

## *Author's Purpose or Bias*

9. The author's point and purpose is brought to the reader through the use of scientific (*a*) research and theory (*b*) experimentation and results (*c*) facts and studies (*d*) theories and predictions.

_____

10. Explain what you think is the main bias of the author. Give two supporting reasons from the selection or from your own background knowledge and experience.

_____

_____

_____

_____

## SCIENCE PRACTICE C

**PREREADING**   Understanding human behavior and relationships is important to develop constructive relationships and to solve problems between people. A short lesson and a little thinking can go a long way toward bringing that understanding into focus.

Armed with the television remote in the left hand and a pen and notepad in the right, I set out to become an armchair scientist. Yes, the TV would bring a world of information and examples to learn about psychology and sociology, the sciences of human behavior. The apparently simple and interesting task ahead was related to gaining insight into the motivations, actions, and impact of people's behavior and to classify examples into the three types of relationships: Adversarial, Competitive, and Collegial.

In machine-gun fashion the electric eyes met and transmitted three- to five-second images of people interacting with each other. Occasionally, the world of animals and an interesting study of their relationships appeared. It was my job to scan the screen for several minutes of random and brief images. Next, I would isolate specific examples for two to three minutes of notetaking about the WHO and WHAT and, especially, the WHY of each relationship. Ten to fifteen examples was the goal. Finally, I would chart the results into the three types of relationships for a research project, correlating my findings to the psychology and sociology of human behavior.

The three- to five-second bursts displayed activities and behavior of a wide variety. The two- to three-minute isolated studies readily revealed examples of each of the three types. However, while the WHO and WHAT were obvious for classification, the WHY was a challenge that rattled my mind like a cage of canaries. An hour passed with mid-sleep speed as each individual study proved obvious for category, but complex in reasons. The results follow.

The adversarial behavior pattern in relationships is characterized by people who do not get along. Obvious or subtle dislike is shown toward each other by the personalities involved. Often, violence or manipulation occurs during the events. Examples of adversarial behavior included the struggle and arrest of a criminal, a prison uprising, and a courtroom trial. Other examples were rioting to overthrow a dictator for freedom, the final scenes of a murder mystery, and an arsonist's attempt to destroy a former place of employment. I observed many examples of adversarial behavior.

The competitive behavior pattern in relationships is characterized by people competing for awards, profits, victories, or attention. Examples of competitive behavior included a beauty pageant, six different commercials depicting product quality or the inferior product of other companies, and the takeover of one food company by another. Scenes from a sitcom showed two friends vying for the attention of the new girl in class. The world of sports was a total microcosm of competitive relationships. Often, sports spilled into the adversarial category. I observed many examples of competitive behavior, and some bordered on the adversarial type.

The collegial behavior pattern in relationships is characterized by support for each other, while working toward a common goal. Cooperation and sacrifice abound. I got preoccupied with the tireless efforts of 60,000 honeybees, each communicating and carrying out the responsibilities of the hive. Likewise for an ant colony. An old western movie flashed scenes of colonial barn raising, an event in which neighbors turned out to work sunrise to sunset, erecting a new barn for a new neighbor. A telethon for a children's disease and the story of a woman befriending the blind in her community complemented the collegial list. I observed significantly fewer examples of collegial relationships.

Sitting back to peruse and review the assignment, I again reflected on the WHO and WHAT information as criteria for categorizing behavior and relationships. Surely, the next assignment would be the WHY of each example or category and probably the HOW. How do we decrease the number of adversarial and competitive relationships, while increasing the collegial? No simple task, I mused, for any psychologist or sociologist, let alone an armchair amateur.

## Reasoning

1. Give one example from your own experiences for each of the three categories of behavior or relationships.

   _____

   _____

   _____

2. The primary focus of the selection is to   (**a**) relate a unique way of studying a topic   (**b**) allow the reader to gain insight for solutions to problems of behavior or relationships   (**c**) show how complicated the sciences of psychology and sociology are   (**d**) demonstrate how powerful the images of television are.

   _____

3. The viewer's preoccupation with the bees and ants was caused by   (**a**) their numbers and natural acceptance of responsibilities   (**b**) their being the best example of collegial behavior   (**c**) the amount of programming devoted to behavior and relationships in nature   (**d**) the tireless energy exhibited.

   _____

4. Write one HOW question of your own and your own answer with topics relating to the existing HOW question in the final paragraph. For example: Question— How do competitive relationships become adversarial in a particular sport such as baseball? Answer—The pitcher may throw the ball intentionally at the batter causing the batter to charge the mound.

Question: _____

_____

Answer: _____

_____

5. The focus of the events in this selection is on  (*a*) teaching and learning  (*b*) entertainment and research  (*c*) observation and conclusions  (*d*) research and application.

_____

6. By the end of the selection, the narrator has  (*a*) acquired an understanding of subject matter  (*b*) become frustrated with a different learning experience  (*c*) realized more questions than answers  (*d*) brought simplicity to complexity.

_____

## Theme

7. Choose one theme word from the selection for each type of behavior and relationship. Refer each specifically to examples given by the author. For example: theme—violence; relationship—adversarial; example—a prison uprising.

_____

_____

_____

_____

_____

Now refer each theme word and type of relationship you chose to examples of events or circumstances in your own life.

_____

_____

_____

_____

_____

8. Which one of the following is the best theme phrase from the selection?
(*a*) gaining insight  (*b*) impact of people's behavior  (*c*) correlating my findings
(*d*) world of animals and an interesting study

_____

Explain your answer.

_____

_____

## *Author's Purpose or Bias*

9. The author's main purpose in using the first person point of view is to   (*a*) relate the difficulty of the assignment   (*b*) encourage the reader to attempt such an assignment   (*c*) show sports in a different light   (*d*) demonstrate the effectiveness of working alone.
   Explain your answer.

   _____

   _____

10. Explain what you think is the author's bias regarding television.

   _____

   _____

   _____

# Thinking and Learning Activities
*Complete independently or in cooperative groups*

## WITHIN A SELECTION

**1. Know**   Choose three favorite selections in this unit. State the author's purpose for writing the selection and a theme word from the selection. Answer each in one complete sentence. For example: Science Practice B: The author's purpose is to tell about the serious problem of diminishing fresh-water supplies, and a theme word is conservation.

**2. Comprehend**   (See Language Arts Practice C.) Review the selection for different examples of applying the word "quality." Give five different applications of the word as presented in the selection in one paragraph. Then give five applications of the word in your own experiences as a customer or when serving the public in some capacity.

**3. Apply**   (See Social Studies Practice A.) Explain a description of the scene of Jesse Owens entering the Olympic Stadium in 1936. In one paragraph show your bias in support of Owens. Be sure to include reference to the historical circumstances.

**4. Analyze**   (See Language Arts Practice B.) Analyze the selection and write a paragraph giving your reasons why you think that Savushkin is the inquisitive, nature-loving, and carefree child represented in the selection.

**5. Synthesize**   (See Science Practice A.) Create a news account as a television reporter of one part of the journey. Include a tone of amazement and a bias in favor of Will Steger and the animals in the report in written form for possible oral presentation or video taping.

**6. Evaluate**   (See Practice the Skills, Language Arts B, Social Studies A, and Science A.) Make a list of ten examples of collegial behavior or relationships. Assess the two best examples with specific reasons in one paragraph.

## BEYOND A SELECTION

**1. Know**   (See Language Arts Practice A.) Record a budget of money spent and saved during a present or past month. Give specific amounts and reasons for purchases. Then project the results over a period of one year. What conclusions do you draw about your saving and spending habits?

**2. Comprehend**   (See Science Practice B.) Review two different newspaper or magazine accounts of water problems. Discuss in paragraph form the problems of each and how you could personally help to solve or improve the problems with specific actions.

**3. Apply**   (See Science Practice C.) Simulate the selection by watching TV and giving your own 3–5 examples of each type of behavior or relationship. Chart your results by briefly describing the examples in the following format:

Adversarial Behavior Examples
1.
2.
3.
4.
5.

Competitive Behavior Examples
1.
2.
3.
4.
5.

Collegial Behavior Examples
1.
2.
3.
4.
5.

**4. Analyze**   (See Social Studies Practice C.) Read and examine an editorial in the newspaper. Present the problem, possible solutions offered, theme, and author's purpose and bias in paragraph form.

**5. Synthesize**   (See Social Studies Practice B.) Develop a one-paragraph editorial serving as "Argument #3" for a 220-day school year. Then develop a one-paragraph editorial supporting the 180-day school year. Give original and specific reasons of your own to show your purpose of persuading the reader. Send your final drafts to a local newspaper.

**6. Evaluate**   (See Practice the Skills.) Evaluate three different television programs popular within your age group today. State the values presented in each program and assess the effect of these values on your age group and then the effect on younger children. Use one paragraph for each program.

# ABOUT A SELECTION

1. Refer to any five selections throughout Units I–III. Cite the selection and explain the theme for each in complete sentence form.

2. Give 3–5 comparisons and 3–5 contrasts between the events and relationships of Unit III Social Studies A and Unit V Science A. Complete in two paragraphs: one paragraph with specific comparisons and one with specific contrasts.

3. Discuss two different teachers, two different personal learning experiences, and two different students you have known who compare and contrast to Anna and Savushkin from Language Arts Practice B.

4. Present two realistic courses of action of your own to solve the major problem in each of the following selections: Unit I Language Arts C, Unit II Practice the Skills, Unit III Science Practice C, Unit IV Science Practice C, Unit V Language Arts Practice C. Explain each problem and the courses of action in the following form. Answers for the first selection are provided as an example:

**Unit I Language Arts Practice C**
Problem: Drunk drivers cause many accidents and death for innocent people. Long-term solutions must be found to control this problem.

Course of Action #1: Impose immediate loss of license for life for anyone involved in a fatal drunk-driving accident.

Course of Action #2: Include a one-dollar federal tax on all liquor and cases of beer to develop a survivors' fund. Equally apportion amounts to the spouse or parents or children of accident victims for a ten-year period after the accident.

**Unit II Practice the Skills**

Problem:

Course of Action #1:

Course of Action #2:

5. Choose any one selection from each Unit, I–V, and explain the author's purpose for writing the selection and one explicit (obvious) bias and one implicit (subtle) bias. Present your answers in chart form similar to question #4 for the five selections.

# Unit VI   STUDY SKILLS

## Overview the Skills

### 1. OUTLINING

An outline is a framework of important information. This framework is intended to reduce longer pieces of writing or information to a manageable form for you to study. The outline helps you to understand and remember information and also helps you to improve writing skills.

An outline uses Roman numerals and capital letters for organizing information. For more detail, an outline may also use Arabic numbers and lowercase letters.

Study the sample outlines that follow. The topics and details are shown in the outline to the left with examples shown in the outline to the right. Notice how the information moves from general to specific or major topic to minor topic in the structure of each outline. Also, notice the indentation and the capitalization. Traditionally, all topics in an outline begin with a capital letter and all other words begin with a lowercase letter.

REMEMBER: You want an outline to include only important information, as briefly as possible.

I. Major topic
   A. Minor topic
      1. Detail
         a. Specific detail

I. Types of diseases
   A. Childhood examples
      1. Measles, mumps
         a. Not life-threatening

Read the following paragraph and then study the model outline that follows:

There are many monuments and attractions to visit during a trip to Washington, D.C. Millions of annual visitors enjoy the national monuments that are tributes to Americans. These include the Arlington National Cemetery, the Jefferson Memorial, the Lincoln Memorial, the Vietnam Veterans' Memorial, and the Washington Monument. The most popular attractions would include the Smithsonian Institution, the U.S. Capitol, the Pentagon, and, of course, the White House. Visiting the nation's capital and all of its sights can be an entire vacation experience in itself.

  I. Monuments to visit in Washington, D.C.
    A. Arlington National Cemetery
    B. Jefferson Memorial
    C. Lincoln Memorial

    D. Vietnam Veterans' Memorial
    E. Washington Monument

II. Attractions to visit in Washington, D.C.
    A. The Smithsonian Institution
    B. U.S. Capitol
    C. The Pentagon
    D. The White House

## On Your Own

Now outline the following paragraphs in the partially completed framework. Include only necessary information, and be brief. REMEMBER: An outline is a flexible framework of information. There is no correct amount of information, but you do want to put in what is appropriate for the major and minor topics.

Albert Einstein may be not only the most important scientist of the 20th century, but the most important ever. It is both the fascination of the man himself and his puzzling work that has created such debate by those who study Einstein's persona and accomplishments.

Images of Einstein the man include the baggy clothes and unkempt hair. That image has been clearest since his death in 1955 through advertisements of everything from beer to books to computers. As a German student, Einstein did well in mathematics, but found the overall curriculum boring. He did not enjoy celebrity status as an adult.

It is his work, however, that has changed scientific history. In 1976, the Viking space probe confirmed Einstein's ideas about the warping of space and positions of stars. His so-called rings in space theory has been proven, and also the Theory of Relativity. This theory dealt with gravity and two dense stars. His General Theory says that space is curved. Most likely, it is the $E = mc^2$ formula related to what is called quantum mechanics that links most people with Einstein, even though the formula is difficult to understand.

I. Albert Einstein
  A. Images of the man
    1. Baggy clothes and unkempt hair
    2. Seen in advertisements since his death in 1955

      *a.* beer, _____
    3. His life as a student

      *a.* _____

      *b.* _____
  B. Accomplishments as a scientist

    1. _____
    2. Proven theories and explanations

      *a.* _____

   *b.* _____

   *c.* _____

  3. _____

## 2. SUMMARIZING

  A summary is information in condensed form, usually written in your own words, and taken from a larger source of written or spoken information. Rewriting information into your own words is called "paraphrasing." Like the outline, a summary condenses longer pieces of information, and helps you to understand, remember, and use the information. Writing summaries also helps you to improve your writing skills.

  Summaries can be about anything: books, short stories, magazine articles, events, movies, television programs, and experiences. Summaries can be any length, but a rule of one to three sentences or one paragraph is good to remember.

  Read the following summary of the reasons for attending college.

   The opportunity to attend college brings many academic and social experiences with which to prepare for life goals. It is also an opportunity to move away from home and develop independence. Several years of collegiate life can be some of the most important years in a person's life.

  Which sentence in the summary above could best stand alone as a one-sentence summary? Why?

### On Your Own

1. Which one of the following, *a* or *b*, is a better summary of how the human ear functions? _____
2. Explain the reasons for your choice.

_____

_____

 *a.* The ear is divided into three parts called the outer, middle, and inner ear. The outer ear contains the canal through which sound passes to the eardrum and the middle ear components of the hammer, anvil, and stirrup. The vibration of the eardrum causes the hammer also to vibrate, while the anvil and stirrup amplify the vibrations to a fluid-filled inner ear. This vibration causes waves which stimulate nerve endings that carry sound messages to the brain.

 *b.* The human ear controls the impulses that are sent to the brain for interpretation and meaning. The eardrum, hammer, anvil, stirrup, and inner ear are the primary parts of this complex part of the body. Improper function of these will cause the sense of hearing to be impaired and require medical attention or some type of aid to assist in hearing.

# 3. NOTE TAKING

Note taking helps you to put information into a simplified form to use later for study or research.

Note taking is often a matter of style. Therefore, there is no right or wrong way to take notes. One simplified way is called the "2-6-2" method. This method combines the skills of outlining and summarizing into a clear and informal structure. The 2-6-2 stands for 2 inches of left margin, 6 inches of right margin, and 2 inches of bottom margin (on 8½ × 11-inch paper).

Use these margins for the following procedures and information. First, use the two-inch margin on the left for major topics or questions. State these in very brief form. Use the six-inch margin on the right to list minor topics or details to answer the questions. Finally, use the two-inch margin at the bottom to write a short summary of the notes.

Remember that information is usually written or verbal, but may also be visual or experiential.

Read the following paragraphs carefully to consider the major and minor topics for completing the 2-6-2 note-taking process that follows.

Protection against many different types of damages and loss is best achieved through purchasing insurance. But shopping for insurance is sometimes like shopping for clothing. There are really only a few types or categories, but the variety of options seems endless, not to mention the additional costs. Overall, there are really only three major categories of insurance needs: property, health, and life.

Property insurance usually includes protection on the home and automobile in the event of fire, natural disasters, theft, accidents, and liability against lawsuits. Property insurance on the home and auto is required by the bank that lends money to buy either. Even if there were no loans, most states require automobile insurance. And it would be foolish to go without home insurance, given its status as the least costly insurance overall for such an important possession.

Health insurance is probably the most necessary, and is considered the most expensive. Most health insurance is provided by an employer. This type of insurance usually covers accidents and illness and any associated hospitalization.

Life insurance provides a monetary amount to a designated beneficiary in the event of death. Generally, life insurance becomes more expensive as the years pass. Therefore, it is good planning to purchase coverage during the beginning of a career.

| *Major Topics or Questions (2 inch)* | *Minor Topics and Details (6 inch)* |
|---|---|
| _____ | protects against damages and loss |
| (major topic) | |
| three categories of insurance | _____ |
| | (minor topic) |
| property insurance | protects home and automobile |
| | coverage for fire, natural disasters, theft, accidents, liability against lawsuits |
| | home insurance least costly |

| | |
|---|---|
| _____ <br> (major topic) | most necessary and most expensive <br> usually provided by an employer |
| | _____ <br> (minor topic) |
| _____ <br> (major topic) | monetary amount upon death to beneficiary |
| | _____ <br> (minor topic) |
| | _____ <br> (minor topic) |

*Summary (2 inch)*

There are only a few types of insurance, but each is most important for particular protection. Property, health, and life insurance can be purchased in any amount of coverage, and it is important to understand both the costs and the coverages for insurance needs.

## On Your Own

Complete the 2-6-2 note-taking plan for the article on insurance. Fill in missing major topics and missing minor topics with information from the article.

## Practice the Skills

**PREREADING**   Chances are that you will enter into many agreements during your lifetime. A contract is such an agreement, but how many times do we enter into agreements or contracts without even thinking about the obligations of that contract?

A contract is an agreement between two or more parties that is enforceable in a court of law. Some contracts that contain ridiculous or illegal agreements are not enforceable. Also, contracts with minors or people who are mentally ill are not enforceable. Contracts fall into two categories: express and implied. An express contract is either written or oral. Examples of express written contracts would be the purchase of a house or land, the hiring of someone to build a house or do major repair work, or a contract to work for a company or play professional sports. An express oral contract might include such agreements as car repairs, borrowing books from the library, or playing golf at a favorite course. It is important to understand that any contract can be written. But most are express oral contracts based on trust.

All express contracts, both written and oral, are enforceable because of two necessary components: consideration and a promise. Consideration is usually money and a promise is the agreement to repay or uphold the agreements of the contract; thus, the reason for the express written contract. Oral contracts leave the door open for misunderstandings about the original agreement. However, it is mandatory in understanding contracts to realize that there is so much free enterprise that time and cost would not permit all contracts to be in writing.

Let's extend the concept of the express contract to daily living, and then study the implied contract. All express contracts also contain implied conditions. A homeowner hires a painter to paint the house for $2000.00, in writing. It is implied that the painter will paint the entire house, not three sides or exclude the porch. But think about the number of implied contracts that are parts of everyday life and the implied agreements associated with daily experiences. Think about the implied "consideration" and implied "promises" associated with such "contracts."

What are the considerations and promises in implied contracts associated with relationships and obligations? Consider examples of the husband-wife (working and paying the bills), parent-child (allowance and duties), sibling-sibling (sharing a bedroom), friend-friend (sharing secrets), neighbor-neighbor (courtesies of maintaining property), and teacher-student (studying for tests and getting good grades). What implied agreements serve as the basis for such relationships? How or why are these types of contracts broken? What would be the reasons for creating an express written contract from one of these implied contracts?

Finally, think about the implied contract of people and animals. Consider the controlling group in the implied agreements. What are the implied agreements of man-dog, circus performer-tigers, dairy farmer-cow, horse breeder-thoroughbred, Asian farmer-elephant, or sled dog racer-Huskie? What kinds of punishments are or should be meted out and by whom for breaking the implied contracts between people-people or people-animals? Think about it!

## Outlining

Fill in the following outline with appropriate information from the selection. Be as brief as possible.

I. Definitions of a contract
  A. Agreement between two or more parties

  B. _____
    1. Ridiculous or illegal agreements not enforceable

    2. _____
II. Types of contracts
  A. Express contracts
    1. Written
      a. Purchase a house or land
      b. Hire someone to build a house or make repairs

      c. _____

  2. Oral

    a. _____

    b. _____

    c. _____

  B. Implied contracts
    1. Agreements not in writing, but with understandings
      a. Hired painter will paint entire house
      b. Many examples of implied contracts in daily life
  C. Necessary components of all contracts

    1. _____
      a. Usually money

    2. _____
      a. Agreement to repay

III. Examples of implied contracts between people
  A. Husband-wife (working and paying the bills)
  B. Parent-child (allowance and duties)

  C. _____

  D. _____

  E. _____

  F. _____

IV. Questions from implied contracts between people
  A. What implied agreements are the basis for relationships?

  B. _____

  C. _____

V. _____
  A. Man-dog

  B. _____

  C. _____

  D. _____

  E. _____

  F. _____

VI. Question from implied contracts between people and animals

  A. _____

## Summarizing

Complete the following with specific information.

*1.* Summarize the entire selection in 4–7 complete sentences

_____

_____

_____

_____

_____

_____

_____

*2.* Summarize the entire selection in one sentence using the 5-W pattern of organi-zation. (See page 51.)

_____

_____

_____

## Note Taking

Fill in the following 2-6-2 with information from the selection.

| Major Topics (questions) | Minor Topics and Details |
|---|---|
| What is a contract? | agreement between two or more parties |
| | _____ |
| contracts not enforceable | _____ |
| | _____ |
| two types of contracts | _____ |
| _____ (major topic) | purchase land or house<br>build or repair house<br>work for a company or play sports |
| _____ (major topic) | car repairs, borrow books, play golf |
| contract components | _____ |
| express contracts<br>implied contracts | apply to conditions in express contracts<br>apply to relationships between people |
| | examples—_____ |
| | _____ |
| _____ (major topic) | apply to relationships with animals |
| | _____ |
| | _____ |

questions from these
implied contracts

What are the considerations and promises?

_____

_____

_____

_____

*Summary*

_____

_____

_____

# Applying the Skills in Content Subjects

## LANGUAGE ARTS PRACTICE A

**PREREADING**   Think about the conveniences that presently exist in your home and compare them to past life-styles. Now think about conveniences in the home of the future.

The waterfront country club community of Admirals Cove unveiled its new custom estate model featuring Home 2000, an integrated home automation system. The Napoli model is the first of the Admirals Cove models to have a home automation system that controls lights, audio/video equipment, and appliances. Also automated are sprinklers, heating, and air conditioning. Security and telecommunications complete this list, all controlled through the use of touch/timer devices, remote-control, macro control, and any Touch-Tone telephone.

While projections that 90 percent of U.S. homes will have some form of automation by 2000, an Admirals Cove marketing director said, "The luxury home buyer is looking for advanced levels of automation now."

The New York-based company which developed and markets Home 2000, provides builders with the total integration. The Napoli features macro systems called "I'm home," "Pool Party," and "Jacuzzi." These systems allow the homeowner to preprogram three surroundings to greet residents when first arriving home. It also sets the ambiance for outdoor entertaining and to provide a relaxing setting in the master suite. Each macro activates the lighting, temperature, ceiling fans, and fountains so the home is waiting for the homeowner with the touch of a switch. For example, the program allows the resident to adjust the Jacuzzi to the desired temperature while still at work. The "Pool Party" macro may be activated, which includes turning on the fountain, special lighting and the pool heater before going home.

The system also has a master timer to manage the lighting, heating, air conditioning, landscape lighting, water sprinklers, and pool pump to conserve energy. Another energy-saving feature is the "whole-house" system check whereby all components are verified in the proper "on" or "off" mode. This saves the homeowner from having to turn off each component manually.

Additional features include the following. A one-button security device activates all the interior lights and blinks all the exterior lights of the home. The homeowner can program his doorbell to ring when the mailman delivers the mail or can have the vacuum cleaner automatically shut off when the doorbell rings. All of this automation is achieved using the home's existing alternate current wiring. Existing homes can add the Home 2000 features as well.

## Outlining

Fill in the following outline with appropriate information from the selection. Be as brief as possible.

I. Waterfront community of Admirals Cove
   A. Custom estate homes
   B. Integrated home automation systems
      1. Napoli model
         a. Controls lights, AV equipment, appliances
         b. _Vidio equipment_
         c. _Sprinklers and heating_
II. Napoli macro systems
   A. I'm Home, Pool Party, Jacuzzi
   B. Functions of macro systems
      1. _greets residents_
      2. _sets ambiance_
      3. _lighting, temp, ceiling fan_
         a. Adjust jacuzzi
         b. _fountain_
   C. _Master timer_
      1. Manage lighting, heating, air conditioning, etc.
      2. Whole-house system
         a. _on of off auto mode_
         b. _Check whereby_
III. _Additional features_
   A. One-button security device

1. _interior lights_
2. _exterior lights_

B. _program door bell_

1. When mailman delivers mail
2. _vaccum turns on/off_

C. All features use existing wiring

D. _Add home 2000 features_

## Summarizing

Complete the following with specific information.

1. Summarize the entire selection in 4–7 complete sentences.

_the home 2000 has many features. It has automatic light activation and heating control. It can control sound and appliences. Any house can have home 2000 features._

2. Summarize the entire selection in one sentence using the 5-W pattern of organization.

_the hom_

## Note Taking

Fill in the following 2-6-2 with information from the selection.

| Major Topics (questions) | Minor Topics and Details |
|---|---|
| Admirals Cove | waterfront country club<br>integrated home automation systems |
| features of Napoli | |
| | |
| | |
| | |

Napoli macro systems  _____
                               _____

                               _____

                               _____

                               _____

_____    manage lighting, heating, air conditioning
(major topic)                  landscape lights, sprinklers, pool pump

What is "whole house"?    _____

                               _____

final features           _____

                               _____

                               _____

                               _____

*Summary*

_____

_____

_____

# LANGUAGE ARTS PRACTICE B

**PREREADING**   Have you read a good short story lately? A twenty-minute lesson followed by a twenty-minute reading can change your use of leisure time for a lifetime.

The major literature genres of the novel, short story, drama, and poetry have served societies as tools for acquiring knowledge, maintaining culture, and providing entertainment. Each has its ardent followers. And each genre has its own amenities of form and function. But the short story seems to have captured the top spot as most popular. A major reason for its popularity is the sheer enjoyment of reading a good, well-told story. Also, developing an awareness of the elements of a good short story and the author's life will enhance both understanding and appreciation of this form of prose.

Awareness begins with the elements of a short story. Memorable short stories give the reader insight into human behavior in certain circumstances. Characterization, setting, and plot are the cornerstones for building a short story. Characterization is the portrayal of people, setting is the time and place, and plot is the sequence or order of events from beginning to end. Added to the elements list are the conflict or problem, the tone and atmosphere, and the theme. Again, theme is the most important idea or hidden message for the reader. It becomes the task of the author to weave all of these elements into a style that captures the delight of the reader.

There are many famous American short-story writers. Such notables include Mark Twain, Edgar Allan Poe, O. Henry, Ray Bradbury, and Langston Hughes. For the sake of example, analyze O. Henry, the pen name of William Sydney Porter. Most of Porter's narratives are mirrors of both his personal life and American life at the crossroads of the 19th and 20th centuries. In a capsuled biography, he quit school, moved to Texas, worked in a bank, and published a newspaper. Porter was arrested for embezzlement, and fled to New Orleans and Honduras. His wife became ill, which brought his return and a five-year prison term. During his incarceration, William Sydney Porter was befriended by a prison guard named Orin Henry, hence the pen name O. Henry. After release, O. Henry moved to New York City. There, he continued to write short stories until his death from tuberculosis in 1910 at the age of 48.

Despite a very difficult personal life, O. Henry's stories are light-hearted tales that have endured generations and endeared readers to his unique style and delightful characters. "The Ransom of Red Chief" is a classic story of humorous bumblings by two very amateur criminals. It reflects O. Henry's life and style before prison in a southern setting. Themes of characters caught in the problems of haphazard decisions, luck, fate, and the acceptance of life's offerings are continued in the masterful yarns of his New York City years. Early 1900's settings in big-city America are the backdrop for such twenty-minute reading treasures as "The Cop and the Anthem," "After Twenty Years," and "The Gift of the Magi." O. Henry is the master of dramatic irony, the surprise ending. Read one of these four titles and the other three will surely follow.

O. Henry and the short story mark one marriage of man and art in the museum of literature. Try a Poe or Bradbury tale for added learning pleasure, not to mention the contrasts offered in content and style to O. Henry. The only cost for admission is a little time, an eager mind, and a book of good short stories.

## *Outlining*

Fill in the following outline with appropriate information from the selection. Be as brief as possible.

I. Major literary genres
   A. Novel, short story, drama, poetry
      1. Tools for acquiring knowledge

      2. _____

      3. _____

B. Short story seems to be the most popular
   1. Simple reading of a short story is reason

   2. _____

   3. _____

II. _____
  A. Give the reader insight into human behavior
  B. Characterization
  C. Setting

  D. _____

  E. _____

  F. _____

  G. _____
   1. Most important idea or hidden message

III. Famous short story writers
  A. American

   1. _____

   2. _____

   3. _____

   4. _____

   5. _____
  B. O. Henry, pen name of William Sydney Porter
   1. Stories are mirrors of personal life

   2. _____
   3. Some biography facts about Porter
    a. Quit school and moved to Texas

    b. _____

    c. _____

    c. _____

    d. _____

    e. _____
    f. Died in New York City in 1910 from tuberculosis
IV. O. Henry stories have unique style and delightful characters

  A. _____
   1. Classic story of bumblings by two amateur criminals

   2. _____
  B. The Cop and the Anthem

   C. _____

   D. _____
      1. Characteristics of these stories
         a. Themes of haphazard decisions
         b. Themes of luck, fate, acceptance of life

         c. _____

         d. _____

         e. _____
V. The museum of literature

   A. _____

   B. _____

   C. _____

## Summarizing

Complete the following with specific information.

1. Summarize the entire selection in 4–7 complete sentences.

   _____

   _____

   _____

   _____

   _____

   _____

   _____

2. Summarize the entire selection in one sentence using the 5-W pattern of organization.

   _____

   _____

## Note Taking

Fill in the following 2-6-2 with information from the selection.

| Major Topics (questions) | Minor Topics and Details |
| --- | --- |
| What are the major genres? | _____ |
| | _____ |

How have these served
societies?

_____

_____

_____

reason for popularity of
short stories

_____

_____    give insight into human behavior
(major topic)

_____

_____

_____

_____

_____

famous short-story writers    _____

_____

O. Henry's biography    _____

_____

_____

_____

_____

_____

_____

_____    The Ransom of Red Chief, The Cop and the Anthem,
(question)                   After Twenty Years, The Gift of the Magi

characteristics and themes    _____
of these stories

_____

_____

_____

_____

"museum of literature"    read a Poe or Bradbury short story

_____

_____

*Summary*

_____

_____

_____

_____

## LANGUAGE ARTS PRACTICE C

**PREREADING**  Simile, metaphor, personification, and hyperbole: figurative language terms that any good author depends upon for more effective writing. Like a polished ballet performance, the author is a director of language, constantly choreographing words into a performance on paper amidst a million swirling thoughts in the imagination.

Take a reread of that last sentence above and then take a cruise through the next few paragraphs as we explore the world of figurative language. Indeed, the author is a craftsman. And of all the tools of the trade, including proper mechanics, interesting topics, concise style, and figurative language, it may be the simile, metaphor, personification, and hyperbole that most enhance the author's effectiveness while capturing the reader's interest. Each one of these four language patterns can create images for the reader relating the senses of sight, sound, touch, taste, or smell.

Following are definitions and examples of these four figurative language patterns. A *simile* is the comparison of two things using the words "like" or "as." For example, the author's description of a battle scene may refer to "soldiers falling like a row of dominoes," appealing to the sense of sight. Or "cannons firing round after round with echoes as deafening as midwestern thunderbolts on a humid August night" might refer to the sounds of battle. In trying to convey images of sight, sound, and touch, the author might write: "Men looking as young as children in battle fatigues faced death with hearts pounding like sledgehammers and uniforms seeping with perspiration from nerves frazzled with exhaustion."

The *metaphor* is comparable to the simile, except that the comparison does not contain the words "like" or "as." A description of an Olympic figure-skating performance might contain the following metaphors. "Skating with all the brilliance of an early morning sunrise, the American dazzled the crowd with gymnastic form and ballet pirouettes." Or "The crowd, hypnotized by every twist and turn of the performance, suddenly erupted into a volcano of adulation as the four-minute spectacle concluded." Finally, the medal ceremony might include metaphors such as "a reservoir of practice merged with a waterfall of compliments as the gold medal was awarded."

*Personification* is the author's giving of human characteristics or life to inanimate objects. Examples of personification would be the images of big-city life. "Overworked streets strain with pain under the merciless weight and pounding of trucks and traffic." Or "Another routine of nine to five ends as the city hangs the shingle for an evening of entertainment and good times." How about "Lonely days and lonely nights may be the life-style of the rural outpost, but big city America strikes up the band and opens its arms to any and all visitors once the sun bids adieu."

Finally, *hyperbole* is the use of exaggeration for added effect. A coach attempting to exhort his charges to a great performance in a championship football game might use the following examples of hyperbole. "We've practiced a hundred hours a day for a lifetime, all for this game." Or "Get that heart pumping at a hundred miles an hour for the next three hours." Consider a last example, "There'll be a million fans cheering for you, so let's pump it up and go for the knockout."

Analyze the examples of figurative language that follow, thinking about the images and the senses that each example appeals to, and how you might integrate them into a paragraph about homeless people.

**Similes:** bundled like woolen trash bags, perched like statues on slightly steaming storm sewers

**Metaphors:** stone-cold ground, memories flip the pages of life in Ping-Pong fashion

**Personification:** a cruel and biting mid-winter wind

**Hyperbole:** a hundred times a minute

## *Outlining*

Fill in the following outline with appropriate information from the selection. Be as brief as possible.

I. Types of figurative language used by an author
   A. Simile

   B. _____

   C. _____

   D. _____

II. _____
   A. Proper mechanics

   B. _____

   C. _____

   D. _____
   E. The four language patterns relate to the senses
      1. Sight

      2. _____

      3. _____

4. _____

5. _____

III. Definitions and examples of figurative-language patterns
   A. Similes compare two things using "like" or "as"
      1. soldiers falling like a row of dominoes
         a. Appeals to sight

      2. _____

         a. _____

      3. _____
         a. Appeals to sight
         b. Appeals to sound

         c. _____

   B. _____

      1. _____

      2. _____

      3. _____
   C. Personification is giving life to inanimate objects

      1. _____

      2. _____

      3. _____

   D. _____

      1. _____

      2. _____

      3. _____

IV. Examples of figurative language for applying to writing
   A. Simile
      1. Bundled like woolen trash bags

      2. _____

   B. _____

      1. _____

      2. _____

   C. _____

      1. _____
   D. Hyperbole

      1. _____

## *Summarizing*

Complete the following with specific information.

*1.* Summarize the entire selection in 4–7 complete sentences.

_____

_____

_____

_____

_____

_____

_____

*2.* Summarize the entire selection in one sentence using the 5-W pattern of organization.

_____

_____

_____

## *Note Taking*

Fill in the following 2-6-2 with information from the selection.

| *Major Topics* *(questions)* | *Minor Topics and Details* |
|---|---|
| _____ (major topic) | simile, metaphor, personification, hyperbole |
| What are a writer's tools of the trade? | proper mechanics interesting topics |
| | _____ |
| | _____ |
| _____ (major topic) | sight, sound, touch, taste, smell |
| definition and examples of similes | _____ |
| | _____ |
| | _____ |
| | _____ |

_____     comparison not using "like" or "as"
(major topic)               skating with the brilliance of sunshine

_____

_____

_____
(major topic)
_____

_____

_____

_____
(major topic)
_____

_____

examples of figurative      simile—bundled like woolen trash bags
    language
                            _____

                            metaphor—stone-cold ground

                            _____

                            personification—_____

                            hyperbole—_____

*Summary*

_____

_____

_____

_____

_____

_____

## SOCIAL STUDIES PRACTICE A

**PREREADING**   Remember those legendary stories of knights on horseback and their adventures in the Crusades of medieval history? Perhaps those stories are not so long ago as modern-day crusaders relive those journeys of centuries ago.

On a bright May morning to the sound of trumpets we rode out of the castle and took the road to Jerusalem. There were four of us: Sarah Dorman, Irish and 22—two horses—and I. Before us lay a journey that would carry us more than 3,000 miles to the south and east across ten countries. Nine centuries earlier the same route from northern France to Jerusalem had been followed by one of the most remarkable hosts in history—the warrior pilgrims of the First Crusade.

All my life I have been fascinated by those legendary knights and their followers. With the symbol of the cross stitched to their clothes, the crusaders endured hardships and marched until their shoes were shredded, their tents rotten, and their horses too weak to carry riders. They completed the only truly successful Crusade to the Holy Land. They endured three years of battles, starvation, and disease, and at the end they stormed the walls of Jerusalem and captured the holy city. They left an indelible mark on the history of both Europe and the Middle East.

The kingdom that the crusaders established was to last nearly a century before Saladin won it back. In that time Europe and Asia became locked in an embrace of cultures that has no end to this day.

At the start of the First Crusade in 1096 dozens of aristocrats answered Pope Urban's call to free the holy places from the controls of the infidels of the East. The medieval bards claimed that Duke Godfrey of Bouillon was the crusader par excellence. Their own chronicles reveal that the crusaders were often coarse, blood-thirsty, and fanatic. Yet they risked their lives for a cause that promised only penury and suffering on Earth, and a hope of redemption of their sins. Like many of them, Duke Godfrey never returned home. He died in Jerusalem and was buried in the Church of the Holy Sepulchre.

## Outlining

Fill in the following outline with appropriate information from the selection. Be as brief as possible.

I. Modern-day Crusade
   A. Left on bright May morning to trumpet sounds
   B. Took the road to Jerusalem
   C. Four travelers
      1. Sarah Dorman

      2. _____

      3. _____

   D. _____

   E. _____
II. The legendary knights and their followers
   A. Symbol of the cross stitched to their clothes
   B. Endured hardships

      1. _____

      2. _____

      3. _____

   C. Left an indelible mark on the history of Europe and Middle East

III. The kingdom and history of the Crusaders

   A. Lasted nearly a century before Saladin won it back

      1. In that time Europe and Asia embraced cultures

   B. Started in 1096 with Pope Urban's call

      1. Free the holy places from the infidels of the East

   C. _____

   D. _____

   E. _____

   F. _____

## Summarizing

Complete the following with specific information.

*1.* Summarize the entire selection in 4–7 complete sentences.

_____

_____

_____

_____

_____

_____

_____

*2.* Summarize the entire selection in one sentence using the 5-W pattern of organization.

_____

_____

_____

## Note Taking

Fill in the following 2-6-2 with information from the selection.

| *Major Topics*<br>*(questions)* | *Minor Topics and Details* |
|---|---|
| What were the elements<br>of the modern<br>Crusade? | _____<br>_____<br>_____ |
| What were the conditions<br>of the knights and<br>followers? | _____<br>_____<br>_____<br>_____ |
| What are some facts<br>about the first Crusade? | lasted nearly a century<br>Europe and Asia locked in culture<br>_____<br>_____<br>_____<br>_____<br>_____ |
| | Godfrey died in Jerusalem |

*Summary*

_____
_____
_____

## SOCIAL STUDIES PRACTICE B

**PREREADING**   Most Americans enter a lifetime of work in a chosen career or vocation after formal schooling ends. Consider whether the choice of a boss is a man or a woman, and also consider the style of the boss of the 21st century.

      Today is another interview for that first career position and the outcome is successful. Now, what consideration was given to preference of boss—male or female? Historically, the boss in the agricultural society during the 1800's was the farmer himself. The boss in the industrial society of most of the 1900's was usually a factory foreman. His job was to oversee the workers' adherence to strict time schedules and, especially, production quotas of goods or products. Most jobs were assembly line, one-task in dimension for a lifetime, involving men and women account-able to the foreman and a time clock. But comparing the image and role of the boss of the industrial society and that of today reflects significant changes.

Having defined current models of successful businesses, psychologists and sociologists seem to be leaning toward the woman as the more effective boss. Models of management have shifted from the top-down structure of boss-worker to the horizontal model of supervisor-colleague. Jobs are more complicated in the informational or global economies of today, requiring multiple skills, extensive planning, dialogue, and listen-ing among all employees. Also, effective workers need to experience par-ticipation and decision making in the company to develop and sustain motivation and pride. Process and product are equally balanced entities in management planning for all employees.

Reflecting many of these management practices, more women are emerging as the business leaders in the modern American place of work. This trend is also emerging around the world, placing men and women on equal plateaus of competition for good jobs.

What are the personal and professional characteristics and qualities demonstrated by the supervisor of the 21st century? There is a need for more asking than telling. There is a need for more listening than telling. Praising the positive is in, criticizing the negative is out. The boss of the modern workplace is a manager rather than commander. He or she is adept at delegating authority and sharing the concept of power. Effective bosses care about relationships and how people feel and think. They include employees in decision making and encourage interaction among employees. A consistently kind and courteous attitude is demonstrated to foster both collegiality and public relations. Professional treatment of the customer is mandatory. All of these attributes are considered "good for business."

Of course, there is no way to reach definitive conclusions regarding the victor in the race of the genders for best boss. Most attention goes to understanding how continuously to redefine and refine one's role as supervisor for the benefit of employee, company, and self. Unless, of course, a company of one is the plan for lifetime employment.

## Outlining

Fill in the following outline with appropriate information from the selection. Be as brief as possible.

I. History of types of bosses
   A. Agricultural society of the 1800's
      1. The farmer was his own boss

   B. _____
      1. Usually a factory foreman
         a. Oversee workers and time schedules

    b. _____

    c. _____
  C. Image and role of bosses today very different
II. Current models of business and management
  A. Structure of boss-worker has changed to supervisor-colleague

  B. _____

  C. _____

  D. _____
  E. Women reflecting these business practices
    1. Emerging trend around the world

    2. _____

III. _____
  A. More asking than telling

  B. _____

  C. _____

  D. _____

  E. _____

  F. _____

  G. _____

  H. _____

  I. _____
IV. What good bosses should continuously do

  A. _____
    1. For the benefit of employee

    2. _____

    3. _____

## *Summarizing*

Complete the following with specific information.

*1.* Summarize the entire selection in 4–7 complete sentences.

_____

_____

_____

_____

_____

_____

_____

2. Summarize the entire selection in one sentence using the 5-W pattern of organization.

_____

_____

_____

## Note Taking

Fill in the following 2-6-2 with information from the selection.

| *Major Topics (questions)* | *Minor Topics and Details* |
| --- | --- |
| history of bosses | _____ |
| | _____ |
| | _____ |
| | _____ |
| What are current models of business? | _____ |
| | _____ |
| | _____ |
| | _____ |
| qualities of the 21st century supervisor | _____ |
| | _____ |
| | _____ |
| | _____ |
| | _____ |
| | _____ |
| | _____ |

_____    continuously redefine one's role

(question)

_____

_____

_____

*Summary*

_____

_____

_____

## SOCIAL STUDIES PRACTICE C

**PREREADING**   Conflict and war are part of the history of mankind. World War II is considered the most destructive and consequential war of all time. Take a look at the reasons for its place in history.

World War II was a six-year military epic staged in every corner of the world between 1939–1945. Chief among the sites of combat were many Pacific Ocean islands, Southeast Asia jungles, North African deserts, and many cities in Europe and, at the time, the Soviet Union. This war resulted in military casualties numbering 17 million soldiers! But that incredible statistic is actually less than the unknown and shameful total of civilian deaths. Causes include genocide, massacres, bombing raids, starvation, and disease. To understand this massive destruction and the toll of human suffering requires us to analyze the major events and causes, participants and confrontations, and lasting effects of World War II.

The major causes and early events of the War began with the rise to power of the German dictator Adolf Hitler during the 1930's. In September of 1939, Hitler's war machine invaded Poland and began the domino effect of toppling smaller and weaker European countries. Following Poland were crushing German victories over Belgium, Luxembourg, the Netherlands, Denmark, Norway, and finally, France. Italy had decided to join Germany rather than be invaded. By the spring of 1940, only Great Britain remained in Hitler's path of domination within western Europe. From July, 1940, to May, 1941, London and many British industrial cities were constantly bombed. But the leadership of Prime Minister Winston Churchill and the resilient spirit of the British people kept Britain independent of Hitler's control. Consequently, his plan was redirected to the invasion of the Soviet Union to the east in June of

1941. The Japanese attack on Pearl Harbor on December 7, 1941, incensed America and brought the declaration of war against Japan by President Franklin Roosevelt.

Thus, the major participants were divided into two alliances of opposing countries. Forming the major Axis powers were Japan, Germany, and Italy. The major Allied powers were the United States, Soviet Union, Great Britain, and China. By 1945, the Allied countries numbered over fifty, far above the Axis total.

As the war years progressed, a series of confrontations occurred between the Allies and Axis powers. In 1942 the Axis alliance began the unsuccessful attempt to control many countries of northern Africa. The Allies held firm and, equal to the task, also prevented German control of the Soviet Union and Japanese control of South Pacific countries and islands. Each of these locations experienced long and raging conflicts through 1945 with infamous battles and catastrophic suffering and loss of life on both sides. In 1943 the Allies landed in Italy, and in 1944 the Allies staged the Normandy Invasion of German-occupied France. 1945 was the year of the Allied advance into Germany from both east and west as Germany's government stubbornly crumbled. At the same time, Japan was weakening in the Pacific as the Allies planned a possible invasion of the country itself.

Key events contributing to the conclusion of World War II included German surrender on May 7, 1945, after the suicide of Adolf Hitler on April 30. Japan surrendered to the Allies on September 2, 1945, shortly after the historic atomic bomb attack by America on the cities of Hiroshima and Nagasaki. These were ordered by then President Harry Truman on August 6th and 9th, respectively. Effectively, World War II ended on September 2, 1945.

World order changed after the War. The rise of the Soviet Union as a world power ensued. Germany and Japan lost their military power but, over the years, rebuilt their industrial and financial positions. The nuclear age was born, led by the United States. Many countries were in ruins with years of rebuilding and financial dependency on other countries ahead. What effects of World War II are still felt today? What are the obvious changes in world order today compared to the post-war years? Of more importance is the question of how to avoid a third world war that might be dubbed "the war to end the world"!

## *Outlining*

Fill in the following outline with appropriate information from the selection. Be as brief as possible.

I. World War II

   A. _____

   B. _____

      1. Pacific Ocean islands

      2. _____

      3. _____
      4. European and Soviet Union cities
  C. Casualties of the war

      1. _____
      2. Even more civilian deaths.
        a. Genocide

        b. _____

        c. _____

        d. _____

        e. _____

II. _____

  A. Rise of Adolf Hitler in the 1930's
      1. Hitler invaded Poland in 1939

      2. _____

      3. _____

      4. _____

      5. Hitler invaded the Soviet Union in 1941

  B. _____
      1. America incensed

      2. _____
III. Major participants

  A. _____
      1. Japan

      2. _____

      3. _____

  B. _____

      1. _____

      2. _____

      3. _____

      4. _____
        a. Over fifty Allied countries by 1945
        b. Far fewer Axis countries by 1945

IV. Series of confrontations during the war years

    A. _____

    B. _____

    C. _____

    D. _____

    E. _____

    F. _____

    G. Japan weakening as Allied invasion planned

V. Key events contributing to ending World War II

    A. Germany surrendered on May 7, 1945

        1. _____

    B. _____

        1. _____

           a. Ordered by President Harry Truman on August 6 and 9

VI. _____

    A. The rise of the Soviet Union after the war

    B. _____

    C. _____

    D. _____

VII. Questions to ask today about World War II

    A. What effects of World War II are still felt today?

    B. _____

    C. _____

## Summarizing

Complete the following with specific information.

*1.* Summarize the entire selection in 4–7 complete sentences.

_____

_____

_____

_____

_____

_____

_____

*2.* Summarize the entire selection in one sentence using the 5-W pattern of organization.

_____

_____

_____

## Note Taking

Fill in the following 2-6-2 with information from the selection.

| *Major Topics (questions)* | *Minor Topics and Details* |
| --- | --- |
| What was World War II? | military epic between 1939–1945 |
| | _____ |
| | _____ |
| | _____ |
| | _____ |
| What were the major causes and early events? | Hitler became German dictator in the 30's |
| | _____ |
| | _____ |
| | _____ |
| | _____ |
| _____ (question) | Axis powers—Japan, Germany, Italy |
| | _____ |
| _____ (question) | Axis powers attempted control of N. Africa |
| | _____ |
| | _____ |
| | _____ |
| | Japan weakened as an invasion was planned |
| What events contributed to ending the war? | _____ |
| | _____ |
| | _____ |
| | _____ |

_____  Soviet Union became a world power
(question)
                                _____

                                _____

                                _____

What questions are important    What effects of the war are still felt
today about the war?
                                _____

                                _____

                                _____

*Summary*

_____

_____

_____

## SCIENCE PRACTICE A

**PREREADING**   Join the President's Council on Physical Fitness and Sports. Organizing a program or participating within your community is a postage stamp away.

Developed in 1972 by the President's Council on Physical Fitness and Sports (PCPFS), the Presidential Sports Award is arranged in conjunction with national sports organizations and associations. It is designed to motivate adults to become more physically active throughout life. Also, emphasis is on regular exercise rather than outstanding performance. The program takes about four months to complete, and is administered by the Amateur Athletic Union. It is available to individuals 15 years of age and older.

A presidential award can be earned in any one of 51 sports and fitness activities—from aerobic dance to weight training. Some of the more popular categories are bicycling, fitness walking, jogging, swimming, and tennis. Race walking and endurance walking have also been added.

Some of the Local Councils on Physical Fitness and Sports are promoting the Presidential Sports Award. For example, a local council in the Midwest has set its goal to improve the fitness of firefighters and rescue personnel. Another local council is promoting the award among older adults, using the Fitness Walking category. To earn an award for Fitness Walking:

- You must walk a minimum of 125 miles for the entire program
- Each walk must be continuous, without pauses for rest, and the pace must be 4 mph (15 minutes per mile).
- No more than 2½ miles in any one day may be credited to the total.

At the Federal level, NASA has issued a challenge to all installations nationwide to participate in an exercise competition. The program is called "Exercise for The Health of It," utilizing the Presidential Sports Award. Also, the Social Security Administration is promoting the sports award among employees. It recently presented a program on fitness to 22 nationwide Social Security sites.

If you want to start or improve your fitness program, try to earn a Presidential Sports Award. Or, if you have interest in promoting fitness and sports for others in your community, contact the PCPFS in Washington, D.C., about local councils.

## *Outlining*

Fill in the following outline with appropriate information from the selection. Be as brief as possible.

I. Facts about the Presidential Sports Award
   A. Developed in 1972 by the President's Council on Fitness
   B. Arranged in conjunction with sports organizations

   C. _____

   D. _____

   E. _____

   F. _____

II. Types of activities for an award
   A. 51 sports or activities
     1. Aerobic dance to weight training
   B. More popular categories

     1. _____

     2. _____

     3. _____

     4. _____

     5. _____

   C. _____
     1. Race walking

     2. _____

III. Examples of programs to earn an award
   A. In the Midwest
     1. Improve the fitness of firefighters and rescue workers
     2. Promote fitness walking for older adults
       a. Walk a minimum of 125 miles for the entire program

       b. _____

       c. _____

  B. At the Federal level

    1. _____

      a. _____

    2. _____

      a. _____

IV. Starting a fitness program

  A. Work toward earning a Presidential Sports Award.

  B. _____

## Summarizing

Complete the following with specific information.

*1.* Summarize the entire selection in 4–7 complete sentences.

_____

_____

_____

_____

_____

_____

_____

*2.* Summarize the entire selection in one sentence using the 5-W pattern of organization.

_____

_____

_____

## Note Taking

Fill in the following 2-6-2 with information from the selection.

| *Major Topics (questions)* | *Minor Topics and Details* |
|---|---|
| Presidential Sports Award | developed in 1972 by the PCPFS |

_____

_____

_____

_____

kinds of activities     _____

more popular—bicycling, walking, etc.

_____

_____     local council in Midwest has a program

(major topic)     improve the fitness of firefighters

_____

_____

_____

_____

Fitness Walking Award     Social Security Administration programs at 22 sites

requirements     walk a minimum of 125 miles

_____

_____

How to start a program     _____

_____

*Summary*

_____

_____

_____

## SCIENCE PRACTICE B

**PREREADING**  People's moods and emotions often change for no apparent reason. During the era of Shakespeare, there was a theory for these changes. But today it is interesting to compare yesteryear's superstitions about the role of the human liver with the realities of modern science.

How were moods and emotions explained during the Elizabethan Age in England during the 1500's and early 1600's? Many of Shakespeare's plays use the word "humor" to mean a character's mood of all varieties from melancholy to amiability to jubilation to anger. Interestingly, the Elizabethan "theory of humors" hypothesized that the human body contained only four elements: blood, phlegm, yellow bile, and black bile. Levels of bile production, according to the theory, were the controlling forces of mood and emotions. An imbalance of bile would create mood changes.

It was also the organ that produced bile that intrigued Elizabethan society. Thus, the belief was established that the liver was the center of emotions in the early days of alchemy. And this vital organ of the human body is so referenced in many of Shakespeare's masterpieces.

Indeed, some 400 years later the liver has not changed function. And to accomplish some insight into those earlier beliefs requires a look at this important organ from the perspective of the medical world today. Maintaining status as the body's largest internal organ, the liver's main function is to assist in digestion. Bile is produced in the liver and deposited in the gall bladder. As food moves into the small intestine, the gall bladder secretes bile through a small tube into the small intestine. Bile breaks down larger fat droplets into smaller droplets. Enzymes from the pancreas then act on these smaller droplets preventing excessive fat from entering the bloodstream and building up deposits in the arteries. Heart disease often results from buildup of fat deposits in the arteries.

Major diseases of the liver fall into the two types of hepatitis and a disorder called cirrhosis. Hepatitis is caused by a virus. Symptoms include loss of appetite, muscle pain, extreme fatigue, and a yellowing of the skin called jaundice. It is jaundice that probably created the false belief in "yellow bile" by the Elizabethans. Also, the liver enlarges and becomes tender with the onset of hepatitis.

Type A hepatitis, the most common, is also called infectious hepatitis. It is contracted through contact with a Type A contaminated person. Also, eating contaminated food or drink can cause Type A. Type B hepatitis is also called serum hepatitis. It is contracted through the transfusion of contaminated blood or contaminated needles. A patient recovers from most hepatitis cases of either type, given strict medical attention, diet, and quarantine for Type A patients.

Cirrhosis of the liver is very preventable, since it is an alcohol-related disease. Alcohol slowly damages and destroys liver cells. These cells are replaced with microscopic pieces of scar tissue. Over time proper liver function decreases, and given enough time and damage, cirrhosis is fatal. Minimal consumption or abstention from alcohol prevents cirrhosis of the liver.

Obviously, the human body cannot function without a liver. It ranks in the group of vital organs with the brain, heart, lungs, and pancreas. What's your theory about the rank or importance of the liver in comparison to other organs? How would you summarize why the Elizabethans and Shakespeare held so strongly to the belief in the "theory of humors" and the liver as the center of emotions?

# Outlining

Fill in the following outline with appropriate information from the selection. Be as brief as possible.

I. Elizabethan Age, 1500's–early 1600's
  A. Shakespeare's plays use the word "humor"
    1. Refers to a character's mood
      a. Melancholy
      b. _____
      c. _____
      d. _____
  B. Elizabethan "theory of humors"
    1. _____
      a. _____
      b. _____
      c. _____
      d. _____
    2. Levels of bile controlled mood and emotions
      a. Imbalance of bile created mood changes
  C. Elizabethans intrigued by the liver which produced bile
II. The liver and its functions
  A. Largest internal organ
  B. Main function is to assist in digestion
    1. Bile is produced and deposited in the gall bladder
    2. _____
    3. _____
    4. Enzymes from pancreas break fat down further
      a. _____
      b. _____

III. _____
  A. Two types of hepatitis
    1. Caused by a virus
    2. Many symptoms
      a. Loss of appetite
      b. _____
      c. _____
      d. _____

3. Type A hepatitis

    *a.* _____

    *b.* _____

    *c.* _____

4. _____

    *a.* _____

    *b.* _____

5. Most hepatitis patients recover

    *a.* With strict medical attention

    *b.* _____

    *c.* _____

6. Cirrhosis of the liver
    *a.* Alcohol-related disease

    *b.* _____

    *c.* _____

    *d.* _____
    *e.* Minimum consumption of alcohol prevents cirrhosis

IV. Questions relating to the liver
    A. How does the liver rank in importance with brain, heart, lungs, pancreas?

    B. _____

## Summarizing

Complete the following with specific information.

*1.* Summarize the entire selection in 4–7 complete sentences.

_____

_____

_____

_____

_____

_____

_____

*2.* Summarize the entire selection in one sentence using the 5-W pattern of organization.

_____

_____

_____


## Note Taking

Fill in the following 2-6-2 with information from the selection.

| *Major Topics (questions)* | *Minor Topics and Details* |
|---|---|
| Elizabethan Age and Shakespeare | plays refer to "humor" |
| | people believed in the "theory of humors" |
| | _____ |
| | _____ |
| | _____ |
| _____ (major topic) | largest internal organ |
| | main function is to aid in digestion |
| | _____ |
| | _____ |
| | _____ |
| _____ (major topic) | enzymes prevent excessive fat from entering the bloodstream |
| | _____ |
| _____ (major topic) | two types of hepatitis and cirrhosis |
| causes and symptoms of hepatitis | caused by a virus |
| | _____ |
| | _____ |
| | _____ |
| Type A hepatitis | most common type also called infectious |
| | _____ |
| | _____ |

_____   also called serum hepatitis
(major topic)

   _____

   both types result in recovery

   _____

_____   very preventable—alcohol related
(major topic)

   _____

   _____

questions about the   _____
  liver

   _____

   _____

*Summary*

_____

_____

_____

## SCIENCE PRACTICE C

**PREREADING**  Few environmental threats equal the possible damage from the depletion of the ozone layer in the atmosphere. Now is the time for action and solutions.

Picture a well-known west or east coast beach on a sunny 80-degree day twenty-five to fifty years from now. Once a tanning and recreation attraction brimming with sun worshipers, it is now reduced to a mere scattering of hardy souls—people who naively or brazenly defy the sun's lethal ultraviolet rays and risk serious damage to personal health.

The reason for such prospect: ozone depletion. That much-needed ozone layer of the earth's stratosphere is being eaten away by a barrage of man-made chemicals. These agents alter the composition of ozone, resulting in holes or openings in this layer above the earth's surface. These openings deprive the ozone of its blocking ability as ultraviolet rays then follow a direct path from the sun to locations on earth below. The first known discovery of such a location was in 1985 over Antarctica. Scientists believe that additional openings may occur soon over other locations in both hemispheres.

The process of ozone breakdown is a chemistry lesson of CFC, ClO, and UV. CFC stands for chlorofluorocarbons. These are chemicals used worldwide in refrigeration, air conditioning, cleaning solvents, plastics manufacturing, and aerosol products. Once released into air, the CFC's drift to the ozone layer, which is a gaseous form of oxygen. A molecule of ozone is comprised of three atoms of oxygen. These are the molecules that absorb and block UV's (ultraviolet rays) from reaching the earth. CFC's attack the ozone molecules in Pac-man fashion, destroying one of the oxygen atoms and taking its place in the molecule. Thus, instead of three parts oxygen, the molecule becomes two parts oxygen and one part chlorine. The new molecule is now called ClO or chlorine monoxide. The buildup of concentrated areas of ClO depletes ozone and results in the openings in the atmosphere. ClO does not absorb or block UV's.

The problem of ultraviolet rays reaching earth is a biology lesson of hazardous causes and effects for all life forms. Human health is affected by UV's in many ways. These radiation rays cause cataracts and blindness, alteration of DNA and skin cancer, and a breakdown in the immunity system that fights disease. Nature and the food chain could receive the brunt of UV damage, given the lack of any defense. UV's can reduce crop production by interfering with normal photosynthesis. Also, the destruction of tiny ocean plants and animals that begin the food chain for marine life results in reduced fish supplies. Finally, other defenseless animals and insects that live by day will suffer the life-threatening effects of ultraviolet rays.

Clearly, ozone depletion requires attention and action. No reversal of current ozone depletion is possible. Many countries, including the United States, now maintain consistent monitoring of the ozone layer through satellite pictures. Banding together through international agreements, nations plan and act to discontinue the production and use of CFC products. Stepped-up research initiatives strive to develop alternative chemicals that perform CFC functions without damaging the environment. An attempt to accomplish an all-out ban on the use of CFC into the 21st century is under way. However, such an attempt may be somewhat ideal. The problem of CFC's, ClO, and UV's is man-made, and finding immediate action plans and solutions will be no picnic or day at the beach. Indeed, a sad sight will be a scene showing that the "surf is up," but the beach is abandoned.

## Outlining

Fill in the following outline with appropriate information from the selection. Be as brief as possible.

I. Ozone depletion
   A. Ozone is the much-needed layer of the stratosphere
      1. Being eaten away by man-made chemicals
   B. Composition of ozone changes
      1. Results in holes or openings in stratosphere

      a. _____

      b. _____
      c. Scientists expect additional openings
  II. Process of ozone breakdown
    A. Chemistry lesson of CFC, ClO, UV
    B. CFC stands for chlorofluorocarbons

      1. _____

        a. _____

        b. _____

        c. _____

        d. _____
        e. New molecule is two parts oxygen—one part chlorine
    C. ClO stands for new molecule, chlorine monoxide

      1. _____

      2. _____
      3. ClO does not block or absorb UV's—ultraviolet rays

III. _____
    A. Human health affected by UV's

      1. _____

      2. _____

      3. _____

    B. _____
      1. Reduce crop production

        a. _____
      2. Destruction of tiny ocean plants and animals

        a. _____

      3. _____
  IV. Attention and action required
    A. No reversal of current depletion possible
    B. United States and other countries now monitoring ozone
      1. Satellite pictures

    C. _____

      1. _____

    D. _____

      1. _____
      2. Without damaging the environment

E. _____
   1. May be somewhat ideal
F. Problem is here and requires solutions

## Summarizing

Complete the following with specific information.

*1.* Summarize the entire selection in 4–7 complete sentences.

_____
_____
_____
_____
_____
_____
_____

*2.* Summarize the entire selection in one sentence using the 5-W pattern of organization.

_____
_____
_____

## Note Taking

Fill in the following 2-6-2 with information from the selection.

| *Major Topics (questions)* | *Minor Topics and Details* |
| --- | --- |
| What is ozone depletion? | earth's stratosphere being eaten away |
| | _____ |
| | _____ |
| | _____ |
| | _____ |
| | _____ |
| _____ | chemistry lesson of CFC, ClO, UV |
| (major topic) | |

chlorofluorocarbon
   sources                       _____

chlorofluorocarbon
   effects                       drift to the ozone layer upon release

_____

_____

new molecule formed called ClO

chlorine monoxide            _____

_____

_____

_____    cause cataracts and blindness

(major topic)

_____

_____

UV damage to nature       _____

_____

animals and insects that live by day affected

action needed                United States and other countries monitor satellite
                                   pictures taken of ozone layer

_____

_____

_____

_____

solutions and plans difficult to do

*Summary*

_____

_____

_____

# Thinking and Learning Activities
*Complete independently or in cooperative groups*

## WITHIN A SELECTION

**1. Know** (See Unit VI Practice the Skills selection, Unit III Science A, and Unit V Science A.) Tell about the implied contracts in both science selections in summary form for each selection.

**2. Comprehend**   (See Unit VI Language Arts B and Unit III Language Arts C.) Identify the short-story elements and examples in Unit III Language Arts C in one outline.

**3. Apply**   (See Unit VI Social Studies C and Unit III Social Studies C.) Practice completing a 2-6-2 note-taking activity for World War I that compares to that completed for World War II in this unit.

**4. Analyze**   (See Unit VI Science C, Unit II Social Studies B, Unit II Science C, Unit IV Science A, and Unit V Science B.) Write a brief one-sentence summary of each selection. Then arrange them in an order of most important to least important problem in a list of 1–5.

**5. Synthesize**   (See Unit VI Language Arts Practice C.) Fill in the following outline with one example from the selection next to each A and original examples of your own next to each B and C.

I.  Simile

    A. _____

    B. _____

    C. _____

II.  Metaphor

    A. _____

    B. _____

    C. _____

III.  Personification

    A. _____

    B. _____

    C. _____

IV.  Hyperbole

    A. _____

    B. _____

    C. _____

**6. Evaluate**   (See all ten selections in this unit.) Rate your interest in the ten selections on a scale of 1–10 from most interest to least interest. Then write a summary of a few reasons for your choice for #1 and #10.

## BEYOND A SELECTION

**1. Know**   (See Social Studies Practice A.) Tell of a journey from a newspaper or magazine article, or a television documentary, and summarize it in one well-written paragraph.

**2. Comprehend**   (See Science Practice B.) Locate the final sentence of the selection, which is a question, and summarize an answer in one well-written paragraph.

**3. Apply**   (See Science Practice A.) Apply for information to join the President's Council on Physical Fitness and Sports by writing to the agency in Washington, D.C.

**4. Analyze**   (See Practice the Skills). Contrast two implied contracts involving people you know. Summarize the conditions, the agreements, the consideration, and the promises. For example, an implied contract might exist between you and a coach at school. The implied agreement might be that you will attend school regularly, maintain grades, and be at practice on time. The consideration is some regular schedule of playing time, and the promise is to give a 100% effort during that playing time.

**5. Synthesize**   (See Social Studies Practice B.) Fantasize that you are the boss of a major company. Write an informational outline that informs workers how a problem of your choice is solved in the company.
      For example, the problem for solution is employee tardiness. The following outline provides information for solving the problem.

   I. Information for solving worker tardiness
      A. Employee submits summary of reasons to coworkers upon 3rd tardiness in calendar month
      B. Employee provides coffee and donuts for immediate coworkers for each tardiness per month
      C. Employee loses break time for one week upon 3rd tardiness
      D. Employee loses equivalent hourly wages for the second month of 3 times tardy

**6. Evaluate**   (See Language Arts Practice B.) Research and compare biographical information of Poe with that of O. Henry. Assess which author had the more difficult life in summary form with reasons to support your findings.

## ABOUT A SELECTION

1. Watch a documentary on television related to a problem like the ozone depletion. Complete a 2-6-2 of the program.
2. Locate the September, 1989, issue of *National Geographic.* Outline the journey of the modern-day crusaders from the selection.
3. Read two of the O. Henry short stories listed in the selection. Write a summary of the elements, including dramatic irony, that O. Henry uses in each story.
4. Choose the topic of a burning skyscraper or an opening-day baseball game. Write a descriptive paragraph, using at least one example of each of the four figurative-language patterns.
5. Choose one of the completed outlines from the ten selections in the unit and rewrite the outline into sentence and paragraph form without referring to the original text.
6. Summarize three positives and three negatives for living in such luxury as that depicted in the homes of the future.

7. Scan selections in this book for examples of similies, metaphors, personification, and hyperbole. Give the selection and copy the examples into the following outline.

I. Examples of figurative language from Advanced Reading Skills
   A. Simile
       1. Selection _____

           a. Example _____

           _____

   B. Metaphor
       1. Selection _____

           a. Example _____

           _____

   C. Personification
       1. Selection _____

           a. Example _____

           _____

   D. Hyperbole
       1. Selection _____

           a. Example _____

           _____